The C.A.L.M.I.N.G.

Method to passing
your LMSW/LCSW Exam

By Alona Perlin

C. Comprehend the information

A. Arrange the content into categories

L. Learn more information

M. Master what you're learning

I. Imagine what you're learning

N. Note strategies and content

G. Gain results

WHAT IS THE C.A.L.M.I.N.G. METHOD?

I've developed the CALMING METHOD, based on my success with my tutoring clients.

C. - Comprehend the information. = You need to comprehend the information in order to be able to apply it to questions on the exam. If you don't understand the information, you may have the ability to guess at the answers, but you won't fully know what the right answer choice is. Therefore, you won't feel confident in answering questions.

A- Arrange the content into categories: Ex. Code of Ethics, Recall, Safety, Application. If it's a theory, identify the type of theory it is: Cognitive Theory /Social Theory /Psycho-sexual Theory, etc.

L- Learn new information. The more information you know for the exam, the better off it is. Learn as much as possible, so you can be fully prepared for the exam.

M. - Master the information. Become a PRO as a Social Worker. Approach it as if you were helping a friend or a loved one. What social work tools would you use? This information is not just useful for this exam, but also for your profession in Social Work. If you know the proper way to act in a social work setting, you will be a better Social Worker. Concurrently, you will be familiar with the information in the exam and be able to answer questions accurately.

I- Imagine what you're learning! Sometimes, picturing situations, such as theory stages is useful when learning information. If you can visualize a theory stage or a situation that you're learning, chances are, you will remember it better.

N. - Note strategies. By strategies, I mean, the method you are using in answering questions. We will go more into this later, but strategies are techniques by how you answer questions.

G. - Gain Results! Again, I honestly feel this exam prepares you to become a better Social Worker. Additionally, you will get your license/s and be able to achieve more in the field of social work. Social Work is needed in this country/political climate etc. Many people are going through very challenging problems and need the services of a social worker to help them through these tough times. After you get your LMSW/LCSW, you will be able to do more for people and also MAKE MORE MONEY!

Contents

A Brief Note from the Author

Congratulations on your journey to becoming licensed professionals!

It is a worthwhile journey and should be treated with careful attention.

You, as a social worker work very hard in order to pass grad school. You need to participate in classes, read assignments, write elaborate papers and also take part in practicum internships. It can be very demanding! Along with that, sometimes, you need to juggle job responsibilities childcare, family obligations, and other crucial concerns.

As a whole, social Workers spend a lot of money and resources to invest into the education. Now, at the end of the 2–3-year period, they have obtained their MSW and are ready to find a job! Right? Not always... There is the pesky requirement of passing the LMSW/LCSW Exam. More and more agencies look for Licensed Social Workers and some only accept Licensed Clinical Social Workers. You are able to get hired as an MSW, but your earnings will be much less than that of an average LMSW and especially LCSW. Also, your career opportunities will be much more limited.

Therefore, the Licensing Exams are important! I have met and coached many students that have had a horrible time passing the LMSW/LCSW exam! They think that if they review their notes from grad school or study certain books, it will be sufficient. That is not always the case. The ASWB requires a certain question breakdown strategy, a specialized test-taking thinking process and a knowledge of core content areas! If prospective LMSW's/LCSW's are not aware of that, they may have a terrible time passing the exam on the first, second or even 3 or 10th time! Social Workers leave feeling devastated, unsure of their abilities and downtrodden. I have been extremely upset over the number of people that do not pass this exam. Therefore, I began a tutoring program to help people overcome this obstacle. I have a passion for helping people de-mystify this process and to integrate the pertinent content into more manageable parts. When I started tutoring, I began to put all my information into shortened study sheets to simplify it for my students. As I went along, I decided to expand it into a book, so it will be more structured. This book contains my secrets and techniques for passing the exam. I have based this book on my successful tutoring practices.

For those that are devastated by this exam process,

I am here to tell you that the AWSB EXAM IS

NOT A MEASURE of your INTELLIGENCE.

It is also NOT A MEASURE OF YOUR CAPABILITY AS A SOCIAL WORKER.

Again, I have developed specific methods that will help you succeed on this Exam! My method uses fun information, memory techniques, examples and other strategies to help you understand and learn the information faster.

The book is divided into 2 sections: Section 1 refers to Exam-Taking Strategies and the Section 2 is Content.

Please read the book carefully and follow what is written. The foreword is just an introduction and some information about me. Chapter 1 focuses on the evolution of Social Work as a profession and the reason why the ASWB exam was developed! The Exam Assessment is a good measure of your knowledge of the exam and its content. The Answer Key will be provided at the end. You may want to re-take the Exam Assessment later to see how much knowledge you've attained.

A Section About Confidence:

A positive attitude is needed in just about every area of life. The exam is no different! If you think you can't handle the exam, that thought may manifest itself into the universe and prove you right. I am here to convince you otherwise. You can and you will pass this exam. It is not insurmountable!

Get yourself geared up by telling yourself that you're going to be amazing at this venture! You will learn, master information and apply it correctly to the exam.

Yes, it does seem overwhelming at first! That's why I recommend devoting at least 3 months of solid preparation in order to learn and be comfortable with the material. It is useful to study on a daily basis. I know what you're thinking! That is not the reality. You may have had a bad day at work, your kids are driving you crazy, you and your spouse had a fight, etc, etc. Arghhh!!! How can you have time or the energy to study for the exam? Well, you can do at least one thing in one day. Anything that you do is helpful, and Consistency is key! The old gym commercial advises us that: "The hardest part is getting started". That is so true and really applies to the exam. Just do it! Dive right in!

It may be your lunch hour. This is the perfect opportunity to take your book and go over one theory. Or while you're brushing your teeth, you can rehearse a defense mechanism in your mind. Grab any moment you can! When you have time for more focused studying, devote time to more reading and practicing answering questions.

Allow the Social Work Exam to take over your life! It is that important. For a 3-month period, do nothing but think Social Work Exam. Limit distractions as much as possible. That means, no pleasure reading or other leisurely activities when you could be studying for the exam. After you get your license, you can do all the fun activities that you want and then some. That is because, hopefully you will have a better job that pays more money, and you will be able to enjoy more pleasurable activities! :)

I always say that proper preparation is the key to feeling confident. Once you feel truly prepared, your confidence level will increase.

When you're ready to take the exam, go in feeling good about what you learned. Get excited! Approach this as an opportunity to show the exam what you can do! Do not think of the outcome. Pretend that this is just another activity that you're working on and don't concentrate on what the result could be. Kick the exam's ass. :)

A word about overconfidence! This is like driving for 6 hours on a road full of cars before you're fully ready. My fellow New Yorkers will relate to this! If you're a new driver, driving in Manhattan while taxis cut you off repeatedly may not be a wonderful idea. You may get overconfident and feel you can handle it and then God Forbid get into a traffic accident! Even an extremely experienced driver may have trouble with this endeavor. It is similar with this exam. Even though you studied hard and feel sure of your knowledge, don't become over-confident. That could mean that you are rushing through the exam because you think it is easy. It could also be that you're not reading every word very carefully because you think you know what the question is asking before you read it thoroughly. Don't do this! Read every word, as you may skip something crucial, and this may affect the way you answer the question. Take your time!

I strongly believe in Yoga and meditation as tools of relaxation and also improving concentration. Yoga and meditation will give you the mental clarity you need in to absorb the material more effectively. If you're not well-versed in yoga, even a few introductory poses will help.

The pose listed below is specifically helpful in increasing mental concentration. For my male readers, do your best to simulate this pose or choose poses that emphasize stretching. It is that important to get the blood circulating.

Also, engage in activities that you make you feel confident and amp up mental performance. This will further gear you up for the exam. Some suggestions may be doing crossword puzzles, trivia games, etc.

I'm not a Physician and probably not a good person to preach about food, but a nutrient-dense diet will make you feel more energized and calmer, so you can attain a positive mind frame over the exam. Fish is brain food, so you may want to increase your intake of this protein. Carbohydrates, in moderation will calm you down. Don't attempt any drastic diets while you're studying. You have enough to focus your energies on, so you wouldn't want to deviate from your lifestyle greatly. A few small changes might help.

I also found vitamins, like Fish Oil/Omega -3 to be particularly useful in reducing stress. Similarly, Magnesium is indicated for alleviating anxiety. **Please check with your Physician prior trying any above-mentioned foods, vitamins and/or Yoga techniques.**

I also strongly recommend setting a date for the Exam. Setting a date will give you a concrete time frame so you can devote time for preparation. None of us want to pay an additional somewhat $200 because the deadline has passed.

I also found it important to introduce Accountability into your study regimen. If you have a friend or loved one that you can "report to", it might keep you on track when spending time on working for this exam. If not, start a dated Journal/Weekly Minder/Checklist and record the materials you've studied for that day. That way, you will know how much you have accomplished and how much more you need to spend time on.

That having said, the exam also tends to focus on social/political trends, so it may be a good idea to brush up on current events. The reason it is important is because individuals that have been marginalized will be more likely to seek Social Services. At the time of this writing, the most prominent concerns are the Transgender population and the persons affected by Covid-19. The Transgender population has been discriminated against and has been denied opportunities due to professing their truth. The individuals that are affected by Covid-19 will have a multitude of problems, starting from the aftereffects of the condition, the stigma attached to the virus, racial profiling, unemployment concerns, Substance Use, suicidal ideation/risk, domestic violence, poverty, grief and etc. Therefore, all of the above populations will be in dire need of Social Workers.

You may want to familiarize yourself with those social/political concerns.

I know what you're thinking. This all sounds overwhelming. It is an investment in yourself and in your future and that is the best investment you can possibly make.

Don't be too hard on yourself prior to the exam. You know that you studied hard and now you will apply your knowledge to what you learned. The rest is in God's Hands (if you believe in a higher deity.)! If you don't, then believe in yourself and the law of "cause and effect". Action produces results!

I would also like for you to take the word "exam" out of your vocabulary for that day. Think of it as "solving a puzzle" and do not think of the final outcome. Focus on each piece of the puzzle (question) and the completed product will take care of itself.

To reduce **anxiety**, you may want to practice one of the principles offered by the therapy models that we will review. For ex.: "Mindfulness". Mindfulness is a practice of "Staying in the moment". Abdominal breathing (breathing with your stomach) is one of the best strategies for remaining calm. Cup your stomach with your hand and instead of directing the breath upwards, target it towards your stomach. Breath out back into your stomach. "Youtube" has some wonderful videos to help you understand and master this technique better.

Also, "Thought-stopping" may be a useful exercise. "Thought stopping' is used in anxiety management It instructs the individual to mentally tell him/herself to "Stop" when he/she feels the thoughts are getting away from him/her. Thoughts that I'm sure some of you are familiar with: "What will I do if I fail?", "I can't do this", "This is way too hard for me", "I've been out of school too long", "I'm too old". If you find your mind spinning out of control, practice saying "Stop" repeatedly until your mind refocuses itself to something different. It's an important exam and is certainly anxiety-provoking. However, it is achievable. I've had people pass that were out of school for 20-35 years; over the age of 50; juggling jobs/children. It is passable!

Determination is one of the best strategies to approach this exam. The main task is to make a decision and commit to passing it. The root word of "a decision" is cutting off all possibilities. Persevere! You will master this. "TRUST THE PROCESS"; meaning timing, embracing God's plan and believing that everything works itself out in the end.

(Cultural reference: "How Did Luuuucy get into the show? :) Determination. Determination is also the key to passing the exam!)

Having said all of that, let's dive into the content and get started with your preparation for this useful licensing exam!

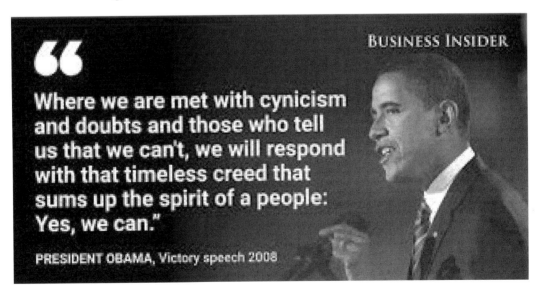

YES, YOU CAN, YES YOU CAN, YES YOU CAN.

Foreword

In ever-changing social climate expectations are spreading expeditiously. The standards that were acceptable a year ago are now subpar and no longer reach the criteria for success

Tension accumulates and for some, anxiety becomes a natural but unacceptable lifestyle. Social workers are also affected by these complicated standards. Their career course is circuited on the completion of an MSW program, ASWB exam success and participation in practicum employment. This also rests on supervision availability and willingness to guide the SW's career trajectory.

The exam is a good measure of success but the thinking pattern in answer formation is not always consistent with the pattern of thought that is used in the comprehension of the material covered in the courses provided by a grad university.

As importantly, the material in the exam is extensive and may overwhelm many test takers who attempt to take the exam. Many professionals feel defeated, frightened and give up. sometimes even before they get started. This is unfortunate because the mark of a good social Worker is not the successful completion of the exam, however, the exam success is required to secure most entry level positions in the arena of SW. it is for this reason I prepared a condensed version of the most pertinent points that are covered on the LMSW/LCSW exam. Additionally, I developed guidelines for memorization, using mnemonics, fun tricks and methods that motivate the test-taker to keep studying for the exam.

The idea for this book came out of my own preparation/success in passing the exams. I have also established a successful tutoring practice for prospective licensed social workers. When applying my methods, my students succeed and do well on the exams. It is my enthusiasm in wanting others to succeed that inspired my tutoring ventures and the inspiration for this book.

My success rate for helping others pass is high, which is the reason I created the book. There are other books on the market that are useful, and my system is different. I will synthesize the crucial points to focus on, which will help you understand exam priorities and the pertinent content. So, if you're ready, let's get started and venture out into the world of AWSB preparation.

SECTION 1

EXAM-TAKING STRATEGIES:

Chapter 1

Nuts and Bolts of exam Success

Just like the NBC info and campaign, « the more you know, the better it is.... »For the exam,

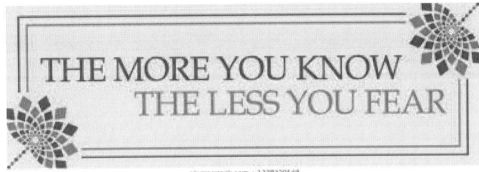

Points to Consider:

Constructive Points:

1. Do not take the exam as a practice test; You may be good at test taking but this exam is specifically designed for social work professionals. You need to be proficient in all content areas covered on the exam and comfortable in applying the information readily. Moreover, if you happen not to pass, it may make you feel discouraged about re-taking the next exam.

2. Focused reading is crucial for comprehension. (This means reading every word for every question and reading each word of the 4 possible answers. (Skimming doesn't

work). The exam is <u>written at a graduate-reading level,</u> so *if you're not a reader, you need to try to become one. Engaging in reading activity is using a muscle. Practicing reading this material, as well as reading answers and questions will get you geared up for reading information on the exam.*

The exam requires reading comprehension, so it is important to understand what you're reading and what the question is asking of you. If English is not your first language or you have a learning disability, you may want to ask for a type of accommodation so you can have more time, in which to take the exam.

3. Digest each question and answers - just like prior standardized exams which you may have taken, the answer is usually embedded in the question; Definitions/recall questions are different, but they are not a major portion of the exam.

4. Treat each question separately; a question given in a latter part of the exam has nothing to do with a former question even though the content areas may seem similar. Do not compare the questions

5.   Once you dissect each question with the corresponding answers and arrive at an answer, do not go back and change the answers - It may seem tempting but is not desirable (The key word here is dissect - meaning to chew up the pertinent information in the question and answer and produce an answer from the content of and also the application knowledge you accumulated while preparing for the exam)

6. Pay attention to key words and phrases: For example, the client's age, symptoms, length of sessions (such as - initial session middle session, ending point etc.)

    For ex. if a client is 88-years old, but is mentally alert, Respect Self-Determination.
    If a client is 88-years old, but is diagnosed with Alzheimer's disease, you will need a family member/legal guardian to advocate for him/her make informed decisions on his/her behalf.

7. Look out for key words: These are the words that stand out: For examples: Very, excessively, extremely, convince, talk the client into ... and etc. In the same vein, look out that words that are "strong".... For example: "It is never a good idea to discourage

the client from something. It is not considered good social work practice to confront a client (unless it's part of a therapeutic technique). Social workers generally do not force, convince a client into any decision (barring emergency matters, such as child abuse, homicide or suicide.)

8. By the same token, watch out for content words such as, First, But, except, LEAST ... etc. If you miss these words, it could throw off how you answer the question.

9. There is no pattern to the answers. In other words, if you feel that the first 3 questions were choice A, it does not mean it's incorrect because every answer can't be A. Do not approach the exam in this way. Choose the best possible answer and not by how many times an answer appears in the questions.

10. Read EVERY word and don't over think the questions and answers. In other words, do not assume, imply, add information that's not there. Don't base the exam on emotional/personal beliefs. This is usually not how the Exam Designers will want you to answer questions.

Approach the questions in this exam as a legal document. Every word is literal and specific. There is nothing in a legal document that means something else. Everything is absolutely 100 % clear.

11. Do not use your vocational or school experience as a basis for answering questions on this exam. The reason is that your agency may be doing things incorrectly or for the sake of convenience and not according to the Code of Ethics. You must base your answers on the Code of Ethics and not what you experienced at the workplace.

12. Some situations might be "normal" and "developmentally-appropriate". By this I mean, not every situation is going to require an Assessment, intervention, etc. It is possible that some clients will come to you without a lack of awareness about a certain subject. Therefore, your answer is going to be "Provide Psycho-education for the client".

On the whole, the exam is very nuanced, so it is impossible to predict every possible type of scenario you can get. I've identified certain trends that I have seen based on

the type of questions that I have encountered. Subsequently, I will review certain common questions that may appear.

In addition, I will give you the types of scenarios that are possible and show you how the situation may translate itself to the exam; Watch out for this tactic: The approach/ and its translation to the exam.

The Overall bases for answering questions:

1. It is crucial to orient all your answers on the Code of Ethics. The crux of the exam is to keep the clients safe. The test designers know that social workers taking the exam are new to the profession. Therefore, they want to make sure that minimally, you keep your public protected. All social work practitioners adhere to this code in applying evidence-based practices to their clients. (Evidence-based practices - proven practices.)

2. The other main role of the Social Worker in any given social work situation is "to do no harm"! Just as in the medical profession, Hippocrates in the Hippocratic Oath postulated: "The Primary goal of the medical provider is to cause no harm or damage to the patient", the same way the Social Worker must make sure not to do any harm to the client. Avoiding harm means following the Code of Ethics, not taking advantage to the clients' vulnerability and protecting clients' rights at all times.

Health and safety are paramount to serving clients. If there is suspicion of abuse (bruises, marks, cuts), REPORT! If a situation requires medical intervention, suggest that first. For ex. If a woman is in her 50's and finds it painful to have sex with her husband, a medical evaluation should come FIRST. The woman's issue could be related to menopause or another gynecological condition. Therefore, you don't need to Assess the relationship with her husband FIRST. You need to refer her for a medical evaluation to rule out a medical diagnosis.

Commit to the client for the duration of treatment.

You cannot push off the client to another co-worker, agency, support group. It is also not a good idea to offer the client literature/information (brochures, etc.) FIRST. The

14

client came to you for a reason. They can usually look up the information online, in a book, etc. Offering the client literature is almost equivalent to not dealing with the client directly.

The exceptions for not engaging in sessions are:

The client is testing boundaries continuously (In this scenario, setting clear boundaries will be expected) ; the client is inebriated, the client is not paying for sessions (after being offered a sliding scale) , objectives are met ; you are sued by the client or you or the client move and it is difficult for you to see each other; you are unable to provide the services that a client needs (in that case you would explain and refer a client to another program/professional.); We will get into these scenarios more in depth in later chapters, but these are the overarching points.

Keep in mind that the client came to you, so you need to do your best to stay with him/her as long as they need you. (Doing the opposite may result in a sense of rejection/abandonment and also liability concerns. The Code makes a reference to abandonment of clients, so it is important to keep that in mind.)

3. Many of your questions are going to be situational, in nature. In other words, you will be presented with a problem (Ex. A client comes to you with x, ...amount and you will be expected to solve them.). The questions will want you to approach the situation, as a FIRST intervention; NEXT, BEST, SHOULD, etc. When you see a question that states "WHAT SHOULD A SW DO FIRST", you should prioritize the situation. In other words, put the situation in the order of importance. For example: if a client is severely distressed, had multiple losses, has been drinking; you would prioritize "Suicide Risk Assessment" in lieu of "Assessing alcohol consumption" or "Acknowledging the client's feelings." The reason is because SUICIDE is more imminent than substance use/abuse.

Similarly, if a client came to you and spoke about alcohol consumption, as well as economic problems, you would prioritize "Alcohol consumption" as a primary intervention. The reason for that is because Alcohol is a medical disease and has the potential to severely damage/kill the client. While resources are important, they are more controllable than a situation with a substance abuse problem. Remember, PRIORITY of the issue - is KEY!

4. You should also look out for trigger words, such as "angry", "frustrated", "upset". If you see that in the stem of the question your client displays one of these feeling-states, you should focus on that. Do not do something that will make him/her more frustrated/upset. Also, if they are upset, there may be other situations triggering the feeling, you would want to pinpoint where the feeling came from (environmental situation; internal situation). In some cases, when the problem may be internal (ex. hallucinations), you may need to refer the client for a Psychiatric Evaluation.

   In other instances, you should mirror/validate their feeling-states and based on the other portion of the question, use appropriate techniques to make them feel at ease about their situation.

   If the client is overflowing with problems, you would need to partialize them. Partializing: - "Partialize" - memory trick/think Parts": means asking the client which problem the client would like to discuss first.

5. Orient your answers towards the principles and the Core Values in the Code of Ethics: The principles present as follows:

   Service: Translation to Exam: Your primary responsibility is to the well-being of the client. The exceptions are in situations that present self-harm, abuse or harm to others.

   Social Justice: Translation to Exam: Social Workers are concerned for the welfare of all human beings. Our goal is to promote justice, in terms of ensuring fair and equal treatment for all people. If our clients are unfairly treated, our responsibility is to ADVOCATE for them. This will be one of the instances in which your techniques will be more action-directed.

   Competence - Translation to Exam: Refer, if you're not well-versed in a subject area.

Integrity: - Translation to Exam: Exercise trustworthy behavior as a professional: Observe the standards that are prescribed by the Code of Ethics when working with clients and fellow colleagues.

Worth of Human Relationships - Translation to exam: Choose answers that prioritize relationships, unless those relationships are harmful. This is particularly meaningful during the termination stage, where you will work on pinpointing support systems, outside of treatment.

Self-determination: - Translation to Exam: Respect client's decisions with respect to choices in their life (ex. choices regarding sexual orientation, medical procedures, pregnancy, etc.)

Worth and Dignity of the Client: - Translation to Exam: Respect the client; avoid judgment. /Assumptions. Everyone wants to feel relevant, therefore, it is important to value each person as unique and acknowledge that everyone has a definite place and purpose in society; Support life-affirming decisions.

6. **RULE OF THUMB:** Do Not ASSUME anything about the client! Do not assume, they must feel a certain way because of a situation; do not assume that you can completely understand their culture; do not assume you can relate to their experiences of discrimination; do not assume the statement means more than it does; do not assume that they mean to say something, when they don't (Clarify).

By the same token, do not assume you know what their medical situation is; Do not "interpret" their mood; - also clarify it; "do not assume your experience is the same as theirs, when it comes to any situation - Use ACTIVE LISTENING" to validate their experience. Also, "Do not judge them based on what you think is happening at the moment" - These are some of the instances WHEN A VERY CLEAR AND THOROUGH ASSESSMENT must be done before assumption. (If you have assumed anything, chances are, you have disserviced them. We do not know anything about a person and must assess continuously before attempting a technique or suggesting an activity and jumping to an intervention. (I am putting all of these in CAPS to alert you to the importance of this rule. You will come to see these situations as you practice more questions, but as a general tactic; Assessment comes prior to Intervention!)

Similarly, DO NOT DECIDE ANYTHING FOR A CLIENT OR PUT WORDS/THOUGHTS IN THEIR HEADS: Often, Social Workers think they know better, but we need to respect the client as the ultimate authority on his/her life. The only exception is in cases of Abuse/Neglect, Self-Harm or Harm to Others.

Remember: A question is like a puzzle you're solving: The sentences are triggers as to what can happen within the answer choice. Look for the context in the first sentence (ex. setting; establishment), also the role of the Social Worker, Age, diagnosis, etc. The problem that you need to solve is usually close to the question

THE PRIORITY TRIANGLE

Maslow has the Hierarchy of needs and so does Alona Perlin. This is what I call my Priority Triangle in answering questions.

In case the Pyramid is not clear, I will outline it for you.

PRIORITY I: IMMEDIATE HARM: Ex. Suicide, Danger to Others, Abuse. /Safety is the first concern.

PRIORITY II: HEALTH ISSUES: Physical Symptoms/Aches/Pains/Sexual problems resulting in pain - take precedence over any psychological issues.

PRIORITY III: SUBSTANCE ABUSE: This is a dangerous situation, in that a client could experience withdrawal symptoms; Medication Intoxication. /Overdose, long-term damage to physical organs/death. The reason why I list this as a 3rd priority is because it generally happens over the course of time. SUICIDE IS MORE IMMEDIATE.

PRIORITY IV: DOMESTIC VIOLENCE: Choose domestic violence, over Substance Abuse. The reason is because the effects may be more harmful and immediate. The same goes for economic issues. You would want to prioritize matters of Domestic Violence over economic concerns as domestic violence presents an immediate danger. Financial issues are an issue, but they are not as imminently harmful as domestic violence.

Technique in Applying to Questions:

1. Prioritize Suicide/Harm to Others/Abuse Over Substance Abuse.

2. Prioritize Physical Health Concerns Over Psychological Concerns. The reason is because the Physical Symptoms could contribute to the psychological symptoms.

3. Prioritize Substance Abuse Over Finances. (If an individual becomes dependent on substances, he/she won't be able to sustain a job. Therefore you, need to deal with the Substance Abuse before addressing areas of resources or employment opportunities.)

4. Choose Domestic Violence Over Substance Abuse: Domestic Violence has more potential to cause more immediate injury/harm to another person. (Safety issue!). Similarly, you would want to prioritize Domestic Violence over Employment/Economic Resources. Domestic violence presents as a safety concern. Once the individual is safe, he/she can attend to their economic resources.

5. Prioritize Psychiatric Stabilization Over Substance Use: If the individual is not coherent and may be using substances concurrently, we need to stabilize the individual, prior to working on the SU. This is important since we need to know if

the incoherence is attributed to an organic (brain/chemical) cause vs. an artificial cause (substance use).

Definition and Signs of Abuse:

Definition of Abuse: any type of mistreatment. It includes emotional, verbal, physical and sexual abuse. It is intentional, uncontrolled punishment and devaluation of a child/elderly individual or a person with Intellectual Disabilities.

Signs of Abuse in a Child:

- Multiple injuries in different stages of healing: (implies Extended abuse measures)

- - Bite marks   Fear
- - Burn marks; welts   - Symmetrical bruises (1 on each side)
- - The story "doesn't add up"   - Hypervigilance

Signs of Abuse in an Elderly or other Dependent Adult:

- - Welts; lacerations   - Misappropriated funds
- - Punctures;   - Complaints of lack of food
- - Missing patches of hair   - Missing funds
- Weight loss
- Head Injuries

Signs of Sexual Abuse: Bruising around the genital/anal area.

Oversexualized behavior; possible excessive masturbation at the tender age

(5 or younger) - Do not confuse it with "Exploration". Sexual exploration is normative and does not warrant any intrusive interventions. The parents that are concerned need to be provided with psychoeducation for this particular situation.

Chapter 2

The Client Process/Problem-Solving Process

Client Process: This includes the Helping Process. This is the sequence in which you answer questions. Please note that the sequence will not apply to every question. You must take into consideration other factors, such as **SAFETY, HEALTH, AGE, DEVELOPMENTAL LEVEL OR PHASE OF TREATMENT/DIAGNOSIS/COGNITIVE ABILITYSITUATION PRESENTED**. You must also read the question carefully and be careful of DISTRACTOR sentences. (I call these DISTRACTOR sentences because they cause the reader to think that the paragraph is going in one direction and then it veers off into a completely different topic. Every word that is written in the stem of the question is important. 1 word could throw off the entire meaning.)

Before we fully delve into the "Helping Process", I want to devote some time on reading the question.

Elements of Reading the Question:

When you look at a question scenario, pretend that you're explaining the situation to an individual that doesn't have full command of the English language: How would you explain that situation to the person?

• Break it down; Put the paragraph into one-two succinct sentence. What is the sum of the case scenario?

• In that, identify the primary purpose of the question is.

• What is happening in the question?

• Who are the key players? (Social Worker; SW Supervisor; Intern, Drug Counselor, etc.)

• What is the main theme?

• What is the emotional tone of the question? (Ex. Are the people involved content, dissatisfied, estranged, divorcing? Are there conflicting actions within the "Main character - the client"

• What is the problem that needs to be addressed?

• **Rephrase the Question:** In other words, put it in your Own words

• Are there any Red flags? "Is the client hesitant/uncooperative/resistant?

IMPORTANT: Use Logic to Answer the Question: Do not put your own emotional spin on the question; Follow Procedures; Don't over think or look too deeply into the fall-out of the situation or create scenarios that may not be relevant in the situation.

• Use logic to answer the question:

RED ALERT, RED ALERT: WATCH OUT FOR "RED FLAGS": (See below)

<u>Red Flags:</u> are GLARING TRIGGERS / WORDS / WARNING SIGNS IN the Question:

- For Ex. The Client's demeanor/ reactions/ language are problematic:

- The client could be giving off a vibe that she/he is ambivalent about his/her follow-up care.

- The client hints at possible harmful actions, such as: "I don't know if I can continue without person X..........................

- The client is fearful/reluctant about disclosing information.

- The client is void of support systems.

- Severity of symptoms

- Duration of symptoms

- Lack of interest in care

If any of these appear within the body of the question, PAY CLOSE ATTENTION TO THEM.

Having said, let's look at the "Helping Process"

THE HELPING PROCESS:

1. Building Rapport/Trust/ Engagement - establishing a connection with your client. Building rapport/therapeutic alliance is crucial. If you don't gain trust with your client, he/she is more likely to go to a different professional or sabotage the treatment. -

   What is Engagement: - Engagement constitutes making contact with your client. It is a similar principle as making a friend - you need trust in order to develop the relationship.

   How this may present itself in an answer choice on the exam: -

   ("Acknowledge feelings/normalize reactions, validate; support, Engage in a discussion....)

2. **Assessment -** taking the presenting problem/history/vital information about the client. Observation: You need to evaluate your client in terms of Appearance, Orientation, Thinking Process, Speech, Presentation, Mood, Behavior, Orientation, Insight. and Reality Testing/ Reality Testing: is orientation to person, place and time, but it is part of the mental Health Examination All of these components are included in the Mental Health Examination.

   Exploration of the problem may be part of the Assessment: - Asking the client more about their presenting problem.)

   Speaking with Collateral Sources: (Family, loved ones.). This may be necessary, particularly if the client is non-verbal, Intellectually Disabled or not mentally alert.

   Psychological Testing: For example, if a client comes presents with depressive symptoms, you may choose to use the Beck Depression Inventory Scale to assess the severity of the depression.

   How this may present itself in an answer choice on the exam:

(Assess. Explore, Evaluate, Clarify, Speak to Collateral Sources; Testing - Referring for Psychological Tests, Gather more information; gather more data)

3. **The Planning Phase:** Establishing goals for treatment: Devising a Treatment plan and collaboratively, coming up with treatment goals (client and professional) as steps to establish a positive outcome. The goals should be S.M.A.R.T.: - S - Specific (not too broad); M- Measurable - aimed at measuring progress in a quantifiable way; A - Attainable (capable of being reached); R-Realistic - (meaningful for the client) ; T - Timely/Time-limited (structured in a such a way that the client doesn't lose motivation/interest ; goals that are too timely (over 1 year in duration or set too far apart; 6 mos., for ex. - may reduce the client's willingness in working on the goal.)

Once you've established a Treatment Plan, the client should sign off on the treatment plan. The client should always be aware of which goals/objectives he/she would be working on. If the client is not able to sign off on his/her own treatment plan, the family member or legal guardian should be responsible.

How this may present itself in an answer choice on the exam:

(Plan, develop a plan; formulate goals and objectives.)

4. **Intervention Phase:** -Selecting Intervention Strategies: This is the phase where you will select your interventions strategies: Interventions are ways to treat/control behaviors, symptoms of diagnoses, and environmental situations. For example, "Medication Treatment" would be a type of intervention, since this is something "intrusive" or foreign that was not there before. Cognitive-Behavioral Therapy (CBT) is a type of intervention that aims at restructuring irrational thinking patterns in a person.

How this may present itself in an answer choice on the exam: (Ex. Provide CBT; Engage a client in rational restructuring techniques, introduce coping strategies, etc.)

Evaluation Phase: Evaluation is an ongoing process; In this Goals and Objectives may be revised.: - For example, if a client is not making any progress, the goals must be revised/amended, in order to better help the client. Also, consultation from co-workers may be indicated. When presenting a case for peer review, it is necessary to provide the least amount of identifying information necessary (as per the Code of Ethics.)/

At this phase, a professional evaluation (ex. psychological, special education, physician) may be required. The reason is that there may be a change in the client's condition, situation, behavior and it will not be attributed to the presenting problem. Therefore, an outside evaluation is indicated.

How this may present itself in an answer choice on the exam:

(Assess progress, review goals and objectives)

5. <u>Termination:</u>

Termination must occur when a client has achieved their goals and objectives. (A more comprehensive of termination methods is listed below.)

You must never terminate treatment or refer to another professional as long as you are treating the individual.

<u>Some reasons/situations where SW think termination is necessary, but it is not indicated:</u>

a) If a client is unable to speak English, you need to provide a professional translator. If the client themselves request a therapist who speak their language, they have the ability to do so. However, you should not make that determination.

b) If you terminate prematurely and something happens to the client, you may be held liable.

The only exception is if you don't have expertise in what a client may be requesting. For example, you are seeing a client as a Social Worker and the Client needs medication. In that case, you may refer them to a Psychiatrist.

c) If a client is from another culture and appears uncomfortable with a Social Worker from a different culture. This is not a reason to terminate, however the client's feelings need to be explored in this situation. If the client themselves decide that they need a Social Worker of the same culture, that is their right. **DO NOT DECIDE ANYTHING FOR THE CLIENT.**

Consent Releases: Consent releases must be obtained in order to access permission to gain information from the other treating professionals of the individual. (i.e., doctor, etc.).

- Consents may also be given out at the beginning of treatment in order to inform the client that their information is protected by HIPAA for privacy. Some agencies also give out consents for permission of the client to receive treatment from the professional/social worker.

HIPAA - stands for Health Insurance Portability Accountability Act; You must know what the acronym stands for! An easy way to remember it is:

Health - regarding health information

Insurance - having to do with insurance/managed care

Portability - the carrying out of the act

Accountability - the service providers are accountable for protecting privacy rights of the individual.

Act - The act that was enforced

The Overall Sum of the Treatment Process:

The Beginning Stage: can be associated with the identification of the problem; this is where the presenting problem will be explored; this is also the stage in which the SW will assess the client's insight into the problem (insight - what is their understanding of the problem);

The Intermediate Stage: may include task assignment; -/ this may be thought of as the teaching part of the helping process (Ex. Teaching Coping strategies; Rehearsal of techniques or behaviors; Replacement of target behaviors; review of maladaptive ways of handling situations) - Resistance may be encountered during this phase.

The Termination Stage: The Completion of objectives; A Review of achievements; Lifestyle changes and maintenance of new methodologies.

Termination:

Overall, termination must begin over an ample period of time in order to help the client process the transition.

It is suggested that a month may be given in order to help the client adjust to the impending change.

A client may not feel like he/she is ready to terminate, although the objectives of treatment have been achieved. Therefore, a gradual termination is necessary, so as to prepare the client for the transition. The plan for Termination must begin from the first day of treatment. The reason is that the goal for treatment is for the client to become self-sustaining.

During the termination, it is a good idea to review the clients' successes during treatment. Similarly, when a projected date for termination is selected, the social worker/therapist must outline a plan if a client encounters a crisis. The Social worker should say that the client is welcome to return for sessions, if he/she finds themselves in a comprising situation.

The following are the only reasons for initiating termination:

- You or the client moved, and it would be difficult to continue sessions together, due to distance. (If the client wants to continue via Tele-therapy, you must defer to your state laws regarding this arrangement. If it is permissible, you need to discuss the risks associated with this type of medium. The risks that it may pose are safety concerns, such as suicidal risks and confidentiality matters.

- The client met the goals/objectives of treatment (is doing well.)

- The client sues you.

- The client continues to come in for sessions but owes a lot of money for back sessions. He/she does not make any plans to pay the money back. This is only applicable if the client is not a danger to self/others. If they are a danger to self/others, you must continue to treat them pro-bono (free services) until you find them an alternative arrangement.

Special Note: If a Social Worker is sued, he/she may use any client documents in order to defend themselves.

Special Situation: If a Social Worker feels like the client may harm them during a session (hit them, engage in property destruction, etc.), it is necessary to escape the situation IMMEDIATELY.

Supervision/Assistance with Clients:

The role of the Supervisor is to educate, support and evaluate.

You should go to your supervisor in case you experience an issue with a client. For example, you are attracted to the client; the client reminds you of a family member and it interferes with treatment, etc. (counter transference).

Counter transference involves any kind of feelings that are triggered by the client. Transference may be a positive experience and an acceptable goal within the therapy model. Transference could mean that if a client is missing a key figure in his life (mother, father) and the SW/therapist begins to remind them of that person, then transference is established. The client now sees the SW as a positive role model for that missing individual.

Your supervisor should give you the tools to handle situations regarding clients, as well as other staffs.

It is acceptable to discuss clients with a Supervisor for guidance, consultation and support.

It is also permissible for Supervisors to have access to your client records, since they are assisting you with client interventions and may also be asked to step in, if you're unavailable for a particular reason.

Supervisors also have Administrative Functions: For example: They may be responsible for evening out caseloads, salaries, keeping track of work hours, time off.

When mentoring a Social Worker, the Supervisee enters into a Supervision Contract with the client. The Contract is an agreement that outlines Supervisor/Supervisee responsibilities.

Formal SW Trainee Supervision consists of Observation/Evaluation, as well as Feedback.

The Supervisor acts as a "Gatekeeper" of the profession, in that he/she decides whether a subordinate is ready to assume the responsibilities of a professional role.

In an internship practicum situation, the Supervisor assumes some legal responsibility for the supervisee; Therefore, the below-mentioned terms are important:

Direct Liability: - refers to negligent supervision.

Vicarious Liability: - refers to potential responsibility for the unethical behavior of a supervisee.

A boundary crossing is an accidental violation of boundaries

A boundary violation is a purposeful violation of boundaries; An exploitative relationship may be present

The Supervisory relationship must:

- lead to a development of skills

- must be supportive and evaluative

- should be a partnership

- Role modeling by the Supervisor may serve as important for the growth of the supervisee.

- A delegation of tasks must be determined, as well as the degree of responsibility.

In the evaluative portion of the professional relationship, the Supervisor should refer to the following model of Core competencies:

The Cube Model of Competence:

The Cube model is an Assessment of the supervisee's competencies

- Foundational competencies

- Scientific Knowledge

- Assessment

- Legal Issues

- Core competencies

- Specialty Competencies (Practice tests, groups, individual treatment.)

- Technical competencies (for ex. Specialized exams - Rorscharch, etc.)

Supervision is addressed in the 3rd Section of the Code of Ethics and may be particularly important for the Clinical Level of the Exam.

SAFETY SITUATIONS:

There are a few possible Safety situations, which need to be handled differently that the regular helping process.

6. Abuse of Vulnerable Populations: (the elderly, children, Intellectually disabled clients.) - If there is an injury of an unknown, unexplained or suspicious origin, you must report to the authorities immediately. It is important that this rule does not apply to situations that are developmentally appropriate.

   For example, if a child comes in and he/she is occasionally dirty, disheveled, or has occasional bruises, the event may be attributable to a situation that is normal, in nature. By that, I mean that the child may be participating in a sports team or playing outside, prior to coming to the session. Therefore, it is necessary to do a brief assessment to ascertain the nature of the bruises and disheveled appearance. The key to seeing if there is reason for suspicion is the child's reaction. If upon being questioned, he/she looks away, shuffles the feet, stops talking, there is reason to be concerned. If the child is over-sexualized (ex. dresses too provocatively for her/his age and participates in sexual behaviors/activities - this is a sign for sexual abuse.).

The target is "Suspicious behavior, unexplained, unknown injuries, marks, bruises, etc.)

7. Suicidal Risk: If you have performed a Suicide Assessment and the client is at high-risk for suicide, you need to encourage them to go to a hospital. If they are unwilling to go, you must arrange involuntary hospitalization. Signs of Suicide Risk:

   - The client is extremely depressed.

   - The client had multiple losses.

   - The client has previous suicidal attempts.

   - The client has not social support.

8. **Domestic Violence:** If a client is battered/physically abused in their home, you need to encourage him/her to go to a safe place (Family member, domestic violence shelter, etc.); If they refuse to go and would like to continue residing with their abuser, you need to help them create a Safety Plan/Escape Plan. An escape Plan is a physical outline of easily accessible forms of egress/Exists in their apartment/house. A Safety Plan is a list of phone numbers/addresses in case they need alternative housing. This applies when they changed their mind about staying in their current environment or if something drastic were to happen and they need to get out quickly.

9. **Substance Use Clients:** If you're not a SA worker and you are aware that the client is under the influence, you MUST NOT treat the client. The reason for that is that you don't know what phase of Substance Use history they are in. They may have mixed medications prior to coming to your office or are experiencing withdrawal effects. Therefore, you will not be able to help them under those circumstances. You need to get them to a safe environment (Have a friend/car service pick them up). If they come back in a reasonably sober state, you can refer them to rehab/AA meeting, etc.

10. **Actively Psychotic Clients:** If you have a client in your office that is actively hallucinating or having delusions, it is not safe for them to be there. For example, if they tell you that there is a plot to kill them and they are not making any sense; they are not responding to any type of reasoning, you need to help them call the Psych ER. The reason for calling the Psych ER is that if they are hallucinating, they may be hearing internal voices that tell them to perform an illegal or dangerous act. They may also be armed and in that case, they are dangerous to yourself and other people. They may also have been medication non-compliant or are having a psychotic break. They need to be transferred to a hospital. (If you find yourself in a situation where you suspect that the client is armed, you must get out of the environment. Do not attempt to calm them down.)

Health:

If the client presents or reports any type of physical symptoms, he/she must be referred to a physician. The reason is because medical diagnoses may produce psychological symptoms. Also certain psychological symptoms may mimic physical diagnoses. We need to know what the symptoms are attributed to before we can proceed with the Assessment process.

It is the same procedure in sexual problems. For example, if a woman complains of physical pains during sexual intercourse, first of all the medical issues must be ruled out.

Similarly, if a man has problems with intimacy (ex. erectile dysfunction), a medical evaluation needs to be considered before engaging in other interventions.

Legal Matters:

If an individual is interested in pursuing "Teletherapy" (treatment via Video Chats); the treating professional must refer to the state laws to see if this type of format is permissible. If it is, then the professional must discuss the limitations/safety concerns associated with type of arrangement. (ex. Confidentiality, safety concerns, etc.).

If an individual is a minor and may be having sex, the treating professional must also refer to state laws re: this type of relationship. The tween/adolescent may be involved in an improper/illegal relationship, and this may become a reportable incident. In other words, state laws have special age specifications for engaging in sex activity. The relationship may be considered inappropriate or statutory rape and therefore should be reported.

Chapter 3

What makes social work a profession (the brief history of the evolution of the Social Work field)

As long as humankind existed, social work was always necessary. The need for social work arose from a division in classes. Class divisions were hugely predominant in societal structures. Serfdom prevailed and an imbalance in socio-economic structures ruled. The concept of « Might makes right « always presided over societal viewpoints. In past centuries, providing for the underprivileged population was usually the accepted practice of the wealthy. The tasks were also relegated to the church and most often, prior social workers were unskilled workers, who were good Samaritans willing to do good deeds.

With the advent of the Industrial Revolution, there was an emphasis on production and individuals who did not fit the norm, were tucked away in prisons and were deemed unfit by society. More importantly, they were « described as lunatics » and were not thought of as productive members of the population. It was commonplace to classify all "lunatics" together, irrespective of age, diagnosis, functioning level. As these members of the population were thought of as "less-than", they were mistreated, mishandled and kept in deplorable conditions.

During the Enlightened ages, help for the needy came in the form of charitable contributions from the church. Social Work was not deemed a formal profession yet. Luminaries, such as Dorothea Dix brought social work to the foreground by advocating for differential treatment of the mentally ill in hospitals. Her efforts were refuted constantly, however, finally her efforts paid off and a bill was enacted to expand the state's mental hospital.

SW came more prominent after the outbreak of the Industrial Revolution. This resulted because due to the development of manufactured inventions, certain citizens began to profit more greatly. However, others weren't profiting and were restricted to poverty.

Although social work was around for many centuries, it failed to be recognized as a formal profession.

The reason that social work wasn't recognized as a formal profession was because some theorists felt that it lacked the theoretical based behind its underpinnings and applications.

As the need for social work grew, the profession began to take on a more prevalent role. Thus, the need to legitimize it arose. This need created a formal educational foundation, which resulted in training, classes and finally licensing. All of the above reasons are the ultimate rationale for you taking the LMSW/LCSW exam. It is to demonstrate proficiency in the field of social work. It is also to legitimize the profession.

The Industrial Revolution Movement contributed to the need for social workers. This came about because the emphasis shifted from hand crafting to machine crafting. While this period was productive and useful, it also resulted in a lack of work for some manual laborers. In turn, it resulted in a lack of work, limited resources and limited abilities to help those in need. Therefore, social workers became more pronounced, as they began helping the poor, needy on a much higher level. After all these developments, a more expanded social work course program started becoming available. Social Work became a degree and then a licensed profession. So now, you know that you know why the exams are so important, please complete the Exam Assessment, at your convenience.

Chapter 4

Exam Assessment

Exam Assessment

Please answer the following questions. The Answer Key will be given at the end, along with the explanations. (**Note**: there may be some repeated questions, but they are accounted for at the end of the book. Therefore, there are 204 questions, instead of 200. Thank you.)

1- A Social Worker meets a client at a party. She provided services to that client 15 years ago. He asks her to have a drink at a nearby bar. She remembers that the client suffered from attachment problems during sessions. She:

A- Avoids interaction and flees the situation

B- Tells him "No" politely and excuses herself.

C- Goes out with him

D- Disregards the past professional relationship because it was so long ago and agrees to meet him later.

2- A man comes in for an initial session complaining of a poor appetite, insomnia and sad mood. He tells the Social Worker that he has suicidal thoughts and can't seem to concentrate. After exploring and assessing the situation, the Social Worker finds out that his symptoms have lasted for 3 years.

What is the most likely diagnosis?

A- Anxiety

B - Major depressive disorder

C - Grief

D. -Persistent Depressive Disorder

3- A Woman has been coming to therapy for 6 months. She has unstable relationships, poor boundaries and a love/hate relationship with others. What stage of development is most likely associated with these symptoms?

A- Pre-conventional stage.

b - Pre-operational stage.

C - Rapproachment

D - Oral stage

4- A woman discloses during a session that she intends to harm her husband: What does a Social Worker need to do after the disclosure?

A- Continue the session as scheduled

B - Talk her out of this plan

C - Inform the husband

D - Terminate services with the woman

5- What does HIPAA stand for?

A -Health Information Protection Action Act

B - Health Insurance Protection Action Act

C - Health Insurance Portability Accountability Act

D - Health Initiation Privacy Accountability Act

6- If someone has 6 months of symptoms including restlessness, lack of concentration, insomnia, general state of unease and muscle tension, they are most likely suffering with

A - Panic Attacks

B - Depression

C - Personality Disorder

D - Generalized Anxiety Disorder

7- You're working with a colleague, and you think you smell alcohol on his breath? What do you do FIRST?

A - Speak to your supervisor immediately

B - Confront the colleague immediately

C - Speak to the colleague further and see what if you can offer assistance.

D - Report the colleague to HR

8- A 45-year-old client comes into session dressed up in a meat dress/wearing high heels and wearing elaborate make up. She says that she hasn't found herself and has always admired Lady Gaga. What stage of development is she likely to be in?

A - Initiative vs guilt

B - Autonomy vs shame and doubt

C - Ego integrity vs despair

D - Identity vs. role confusion

9 - A child hits another child at school. The mother punishes him by taking away his IPhone. The child says, "Next time I won't hit because my IPhone will be taken away". What stage of moral development is the child in?

A - Sensorimotor stage

B - Preoperational stage

C - Pre conventional stage

D - Conventional stage

10. A mom brings her child to a session. She says that the child's grandmother just passed away. The little girl doesn't express any emotions about the death. She also thinks that grandma was taken by the "boogey man". Subsequently, the mother says that the believes the child also has problems because she hasn't learned how to count numbers in order. What stage of development is she most likely in?

A. Formal operations stage

B. Trust vs mistrust

C. Preoperational stage

D. Object Constancy

11. A mother comes to a social worker for treatment for her child. She says the child keeps to himself most of the time. He hasn't learned how to speak full sentences. He has to have his toys arranged in a certain order. He also stands by a window often and rocks himself. The child is most likely diagnosed with:

A - Intellectual disability

B - Mental Retardation

C - Autistic Spectrum Disorder

D - Depression

12. An adult female is confined to a wheelchair. She can't speak, take care of any Adult Living Skills or travel independently. She is unable to complete these tasks even with prompting. What level of functioning is she displaying?

A - Mild Intellectual Disability.

B- Autistic Spectrum Disorder

C- Profound Intellectual Disability

D - Tourette's Syndrome

13. A social worker in a nursing home notices that one of the elderly patients stops talking all of a sudden. She also stopped socializing with others and has unexplained bruises and burns on her legs. The SW's first course of action is to:

A. - Speak more to the woman to explore the situation.

B. - Talk to one of the staff on the unit.

C. - Report the incident to the supervisor.

D. - Report the incident to the authorities.

14. Beyonce and JayZ are seen for couple's therapy. They are attending sessions because they can't agree on the roles in their relationship. Beyonce wants to be in control of the finances and Jay Z insists on taking charge of the situation. What is that an example of?

A. Role reversal

B. Power struggle

C. Role confusion

D. Power play

15. A woman has a problem with her co-worker. The co-worker gets on her nerves and reports her to the boss constantly. The woman hates this colleague. However, every time they meet, she showers the colleague with praise, gifts and compliments. What is that an example of?

A. Projection

B. Rationalization

C. People pleasing.

D. Reaction formation.

16. A famous actor has just completed rehab for alcohol dependency. What is the most likely time frame, in which he may relapse?

A. Within 1 week

B. Within 6 months.

C. Within 1 month.

D. Within a year.

17. A man would like to toilet train his puppy to urinate outside. Every time the puppy urinates outside, the man tells him, "Good Boy!" The puppy responds positively to this training and urinates where he is supposed to. What theory is the man using?

A. Pavlov's method of conditioning.

B. Negative reinforcement.

C. The Law of Effect.

D. Aversion therapy.

18. A social worker has been seeing a client for a period of 2 months. During this time frame, she realizes that the client reminds her of her ex-boyfriend. The Social Worker still has unresolved feelings for her boyfriend. She becomes uncomfortable and does not know how to proceed. What should the social worker do in this situation?

A. Tell the client that she cannot continue services.

B. Continue to treat him.

C. Discuss the situation with her supervisor.

D. Take a vacation to regroup and think about the situation.

19. A woman is seeing a social worker for symptoms of depression. During their sessions, the social worker suggests that she sees a therapist. The woman becomes excessively emotional and tells her that she does not need therapy at all and can heal her depression using candle rituals. What culture group does the woman most likely belong to?

A. Native American

B. Asian

C. Hispanic

D. Black American

20. A 10-year-old boy comes in for a session with a Social Worker. The boy is unusually quiet, withdrawn and guarded. The social worker also sees unusual cuts, scrapes and marks on the boys' legs. What should the social worker do FIRST?

A. Talk to the boy to find out why he is acting shy.

B. Contact the parents after the session.

C. Refer him to a physician for his cuts, scrapes and marks on the legs.

D. Report the situation to the authorities.

21. A social worker has been treating a client for a period of 6 months. The client is an Asian-American woman. During the holidays, the client brings the social worker a box of cookies to show her appreciation. What should the social worker do?

A. Show the cookies to her supervisor.

B. Turn down the cookies but thank the client.

C. Accept gracefully and share the cookies with her co-workers.

D. Accept the cookies but tell her not to bring anything in the future.

22. A man has seen a social worker for a few months. After a few months, he grins and tells the social worker that he has a special surprise for her. The social worker inquires as to what the surprise is: The man pulls out a box and shows her a "Victoria Secret nightgown." What should the social worker do?

A. Accept the night gown and thank the client.

B. Report the incident to her supervisor.

C. Explain to the man that the gift is inappropriate, and she cannot accept it.

D. Explain to the man that the gift is not appropriate and discuss the situation with her supervisor.

23. A man complains to the social worker about his wife. He says that the wife never nurtured their daughter, never held her as a baby and haven't bonded with her when she was first born. He reports that the daughter is now grown up and is extremely suspicious of others. What stage of development hasn't been resolved for her, according to Erikson?

A. Conventional Stage.

B. Concrete Operational Stage.

C. Trust vs. Mistrust.

D. Anal Stage.

24. Which group members are more likely to be a fit for a group?

A. Homogenous

B. Dissimilar.

C. Heterogeneous

D. Completely alike.

25. A social worker is informed by their agency that there is a high prevalence of cases of diabetes in an identified community. The social worker is concerned and wants to help the community. He gathers information and statistics about the cases of diabetes that are in that area. The social worker decides to develop a "Diabetes Awareness Training" at a local community center. What is that type of community organizing called?

A. Locality Development.

B. Social Reform.

C. Social Action.

D. Social Planning

26. A family comes to a social worker for services. The husband and wife don't look at each other. They are sitting in different corners. Their adolescent daughter is sitting between them on the couch. When the social worker begins to speak to the wife, she says, "I don't know, speak to him" and points to the husband. When the social worker speaks to the husband, he says, "She is the one that brought me here. She should speak." Then the wife turns to the daughter and says: "Jenny, why don't you tell your father that he is part of the family too and he should talk". What type of technique is the wife using?

A. Finding an "Identified patient".

B. Blame

C. Triangulation

D. Paradoxical Directive.

27. A man has recently been promoted at his job and has been celebrating every weekend by drinking all day every Saturday and Sunday. On Monday, he feels somewhat hung over, but drinks some coffee and is able to go to work. He has no significant problems doing his job that day. What is that an example of?

A. Substance Abuse Withdrawal.

B. Substance Dependence.

C. Substance Abuse.

D. Signs of Alcohol Use.

28. A division in an agency has just experienced huge budget cuts. Some employees were laid off and the employees that are still working have been asked to double up on responsibilities. There is high stress in the division. The employees have begun to use more "sick days, vacation days and personal days." The reports are not getting done in a timely manner. The clients are not being seen in a timely manner. The administrator holds a meeting with other administrative staff to discuss what is happening. What should the administrator do NEXT?

A. Change the "Sick leave policy".

B. Delegate the responsibilities more efficiently.

C. Hold a meeting with the remaining staff and ask their input regarding their concerns with the situation.

D. Hire more staff.

29. An individual comes to a social worker for services. She complains of many things that are going wrong with her life. She says that she lost her job, is anxious about her finances, is worried about her kids. She also says that the anxiety keeps her up at night and she cannot function during the day. This affects her ability to find a new job and to remain calm in front of her kids. The social worker says: "It sounds like you are extremely stressed out." What communication technique is the social worker using?

A. Reflection

B. Partialization.

C. Listening with intent.

D. Clarification.

30. A social work student recently obtained his M.S.W. He has been hired by a social services agency and conducts support groups for persons with Anxiety. The SW has been planning on taking his Licensing Exam and has an exam that is scheduled for the following month. One of the group members asks the social worker is he is a licensed social worker? How should the SW answer?

A. I have my Master's in Social Work.

B. I am planning to take the Licensing Exam next month and am confident that I will pass, so you can consider me Licensed.

C. I have experience, so a license is not important.

D. I am a Social Worker with an M.S.W.; I am in training to take my exam. However, I am not yet a licensed professional.

31. A man has recently divorced his wife. He states although he has children, because he's socially disconnected, he's not worried about the children's future at present. What stage of social development is he likely to be in?

A - Trust vs Mistrust

B- Intimacy vs Isolation

C- Generativity vs Stagnation

D - initiative vs guilt

32- A Woman in her 40's is attending a work conference. Her supervisor and colleagues share some opinions on a work project. The woman adopts the same opinions as they have. When asked about this project, she answers by imitating her boss's and colleagues' opinions. What stage of development is she likely to be stuck in?

A- Ego Integrity vs. Despair

B- Autonomy vs Shame and Doubt

C- Intimacy vs Isolation

D- identity vs Role confusion

33 - A woman and a child are seen at a social worker's office. The child explores the office by looking and examining toys. He also answers questions readily when asked. What stage of development is he likely to be in?

A - Autonomy vs Shame and Doubt.

B - Initiative vs. Guilt

C- Ego Integrity vs Despair

D - Industry vs inferiority

34- A woman disclosed that she has a good relationship with her husband, has good friends and co-workers. What stage of development is she in according to Erikson?

A- Industry vs inferiority

B- Generativity vs Stagnation

C- Intimacy vs Isolation

D- Pre-operational stage

35- A FAMILY comes to see a SW because they feel that their 6-year-old child is doing badly in school. The little girl can't keep up with her homework, is not making friends and displays an overall state of anxiety over school. What stage of development is she displaying?

A- Industry vs Inferiority

B- Pre-conventional stage.

C- Identity vs role confusion

D- initiative vs guilt.

36- A man is seen by a social worker. He tells the social worker that he's really proud of how he spent his life. He's had a productive career, a great family and great friends. What stage of development is he in?

A- Generativity vs Stagnation

B- Ego Integrity vs Despair

C- Post- conventional operations stage.

D- Symbiosis.

37- A couple is seen at home by a SW along with their 2-year-old baby. They state that the baby is attached to other family members; is demonstrating appropriate developmental milestones and seems content and happy. What stage of development is the baby displaying?

A- Sensori-Motor stage

B- Autonomy vs Shame and Doubt

C- Anal stage

D- Industry vs Inferiority

38- A Woman talks the social worker she has trouble making friends as she is extremely suspicious of others. She feels that she cannot rely on anyone, and everyone is out to take advantage of her. What stage of social development is she likely to be in?

A-Concrete Operational Stage.

B- Intimacy vs Isolation

C- Trust vs Mistrust

D- Object Constancy

39- A 7-year-old girl tells the Social Worker that she is not interested in the opposite sex and would just like to hang out and make friends. What stage of development is she likely to be in?

A- Formal Operations

B- Pre-conventional Stage

C- Latency

D- Genital stage

40 - A boy is crawling around on the floor while his mother is still in view. The mother is keeping a close eye on him and does not let him out of the room or her sight. What stage of development is the child likely to be in?

A- Autonomy vs. Shame and Doubt.

B- Trust vs. Mistrust.

C- Object Constancy

D- Differentiation.

41- A teenager is seen at a social worker's office. He discloses to the SW that all his friends are doing crack/cocaine and are drinking constantly. He believes that this is the right thing to do. What stage of development is the adolescent likely to be in?

A- Identity vs. Identity and role confusion.

B- Conventional Stage

C- Pre-operation Stage

D- Phallic stage.

42- A woman suspects that her child may have been sexually molested. The boy is about 5 years old and is not completely aware of his genitals. The boy looks traumatized and, doesn't want to speak and has bruises on his thighs.

What stage of development is the boy likely to be in?

A- Initiative vs. Guilt

B.- Autonomy vs. Shame and Doubt

C- Phallic Stage

D- Genital Stage.

43. A grief group has passed through the stages of forming and "norming". It has now become a cohesive group and the group members have gotten to know one another. At one point during a group session, the group leader notices that all the members are expressing the same opinion. What is that concept called?

A- Pre-affiliation.

B- Cohesion.

C- Homogenous group.

D- Groupthink

44. A man is demonstrating symptoms of overwhelming sadness, changes in sleep and appetite. He also exhibits decreased concentration. The social worker finds out that symptoms have been lasting for a period of 2 weeks. What is the most likely diagnosis?

A- Generalized Anxiety Disorder.

B- Major depressive disorder.

C- narcissistic personality disorder

D- Persistent Depressive Disorder.

45. A woman in a social work office rats out her colleague for doing what she deems as bad work. After a while, she has a crisis of consciousness and decides to go up to her supervisor and tell her that the colleague has other redeeming qualities. What defense mechanism is she using?

A- Splitting

B- Undoing

C- Reaction Formation.

D- Projection.

46. A man is working with a group of patients who are depressed. He designs a study in which he uses a "sugar pill" to study its psychological effect on the subjects' mood level. He finds that all of his subjects in the group derive a great benefit from this "sugar pill". They all report feeling happier. In this research design, what is the outcome of the sugar pill referred to: (meaning feeling happier)?

A- Single subject design.

B- Supernova

C- Dependent variable.

D- Independent variable.

47. What is the most likely treatment source of someone suffering with anxiety?

A- Klonozepam

B- Buproprion

C- Lithium

D- Prozac.

48. A man starts to work at a social services office. A lot of his job has to depend on typing up reports. He tells his supervisor that he has Carpal Tunnel Syndrome that severely affects his ability to type for long periods of time. The supervisor tells him that there is nothing he can do, and he must be able to type in order to be able to work effectively at his job. What policy is the Supervisor violating?

A- The Older with Americans Act.

B- The Indian Welfare Act.

C- The American with Disabilities Act.

D- The Tarasoff Act.

49. A man has recently left a hospital. He is having ankle pain as a result of diabetes. He is mentally alert but needs help with ambulating around the community. After discharging him from the hospital, what should the Social Worker do NEXT?

A- Explore his ability to make decisions on his own.

B- Assess his collateral resources.

C- Connect him with community and resources to help him with ambulation difficulties.

D- Explore Home health Aide options.

50. A woman is seen at a Public Assistance office. She reports that she is currently living with her boyfriend. She states that the boyfriend helps her out financially. However, he also often physically assaults her. After interviewing the woman to assess her for Public Assistance benefits, what should the social worker do FIRST?

A- Refer her to a domestic violence shelter immediately.

B- Suggest couples therapy with the boyfriend.

C- Ask her about her other financial options and if she only has her boyfriend as a source of financial support, encourage her to stay with him.

D- Give her resources for finding a job.

51. A social worker works in a clinic. A client has been coming in for a period of 3 months. He tells her that recently, he has lost his job and is not able to pay the same amount for sessions. The SW suggests a reduced amount for sessions, but the client is still unable to pay. During this time frame, the client reports that he has been feeling suicidal and doesn't want to go on because he does not have employment anymore. What should a social worker do?

A- Terminate treatment as he cannot pay.

B- Continue treating the client indefinitely.

C- Continue treating the client, while looking for a free clinic for him.

D- Tell the client to come back when he has found a job.

52. A client is seen by a clinic for symptoms of depression. The SW asks the client,

" Charles, if all your problems were solved by tomorrow, what would your life look like? What technique is the SW using?

A- Unconditional positive regard.

B- Solution-focused therapy.

C- "The miracle question".

D- Jungian therapy.

53- A child is walking around in the Social Worker's office. The mother is present in the office and does not take her eyes off the child. What stage of object relations theory is the child most likely in?

A- Trust vs. Mistrust.

B- Practicing.

C- Differentiation.

D- Pre-conventional Stage.

54 - A mother tells a child that she will be going away on a business trip for a couple of days. The child understands that the mother will be coming back. What stage of Mahler's object relations theory is the child exhibiting?

A- Rapproachment.

B- Object Constancy.

C- Object permanence concept.

D- Anal stage.

55- A Social Worker sees a child and mother in their home. The child walks towards the door but keeps turning around to make sure the mother is watching. What stage of development is the child likely to be in?

A- Autonomy vs. Shame and Doubt.

B- Initiative vs. Guilt

C- Practicing.

D- Rapproachment.

56. An infant was just born. He is in his own shell and does not recognize the mother as a separate being. What stage of development is the infant likely to be in, according to object relations theory?

A- Autistic.

B- Symbiotic.

C- Initiative vs. Guilt.

D- Pre-operational stage.

57. A child and mother are seen at home. The child is about 2 years old. The mother holds the child on her lap. The child is very connected with the mother but has started to perceive the mother as a separate being. What stage of development is the child likely to be in?

A- Differentiation.

B- Symbiosis.

C- Anal stage.

D- Industry vs. Inferiority.

58. A woman comes into a Social Worker's office and says that she is dissatisfied because she is not living a fulfilling life. She states that she only goes to work, pays bills, sleeps and eats. She would like to grow and aspire to have a more rewarding, productive life. The Social Worker proceeds by continuously accepting and validating the woman. What technique is the Social Worker using?

A- Groupthink.

B- Unconditional positive regard.

C- Gestalt therapy.

D- Person-centered therapy.

59. Refer to the same question as #58. What type of therapy is the Social Worker using?

A- Jungian therapy approach.

B- Person centered therapy.

C- Cognitive Behavioral Therapy.

D- Psychoanalytic therapy.

60. A clinical social worker is pointing out the in congruency between a client's actions and thinking. What technique is he using?

A- Clarification.

B- Confrontation.

C- Free association.

D- Rationalizing.

61. Two colleagues get into a verbal altercation. One of the colleagues starts becoming very angry and yelling. He says to the other worker, "You are an angry person." What defense mechanism is he using?

A- Rationalization.

B- Displacement.

C- Projection

D - Sublimation.

62. A woman and a child are seen at a social services agency. The child puts an ice cube in his mouth and winces. He has just learned that the ice cube is cold. What stage of development is he operating from?

A- Autonomy vs. Shame and Doubt.

B- Sensori-motor stage.

C- Genital Stage.

D - Oral Stage.

63. A teenager has disclosed to the Social Worker that he is not interested in going to college. He has developed a whole plan of his life after high school. He states that he will be travelling through Europe for a year and will then join the Army. What stage of cognitive development is he likely to be in?

A- Formal Operations.

B- Post-conventional stage.

C- Pre-operational.

D- Identity vs. Identity diffusion or role confusion.

64. A Social Worker places two glasses in front of a child. The glasses have the same amount of liquid in them, but one glass is taller, and the other is shorter. When asked which glass has the most liquid, the child answers that they have the same amount of liquid in them. What stage of development is the child likely to be in?

A. Pre-operational Stage.

B- Conservation.

C- Concrete Operational Stage.

D- Rapproachment.

65. A woman is interested in buying a new Michael Kors dress. She learns that the dress is $800. She is also aware that this month she has to pay other expenses like her exam payment, her study materials and her monthly credit card bills. She decides to hold off on getting the dress until a time when she can afford it. What process in psychodynamic theory is she using?

A- Id.

B- The Electra Complex.

C- Rationalizing.

D- Superego.

66. A woman has a bad day at work and is really angry at her boss but knows that it is not a good idea to yell at him. She goes home and puts on her CALM meditation app in order to relax and unwind. Which defense mechanism is the woman using?

A- Projection identification.

B- Undoing.

C- Intellectualization.

D- Sublimation.

67. A man has just learned that his 95-year-old grandfather just passed away. He was close to the grandfather, but instead of grieving or crying, he says, "Well, he was old anyway." What defense mechanism is he using?

A- Isolation of Affect.

B- Individuation.

C- Intellectualization.

D- Denial.

68. A woman just bought a cute Coach purse for her best friend. When she gets home, she decides that she wants to keep the purse. In order to feel better about keeping the purse, she says, "Well, my friend did not know she was getting anyway." What defense mechanism is that likely to be?

A- Rationalization.

B- Projection.

C- Undoing.

D- Guilt.

69. A whole social services division just messed up on an annual state audit. One of the colleagues feels awful and blames the entire debacle on herself. What defense mechanism is she utilizing?

A- Projection.

B- Introjection.

C- Intellectualization.

D- Reaction Formation.

70. A woman learned that one of her aunts passed away. She is visibly upset, crying and hysterical. She makes a motion above and says, "Please God, if you bring my aunt back, I will give up sexual activity forever." What stage of grieving is the woman in?

A- Denial.

B- Anger.

C- Bargaining.

D- Loss.

71. A teenager has just learned how to drive. He understands that following the speed limit is crucial for safety purposes. What part of morality development theory is he in?

A- Pre-conventional morality.

B- Post conventional morality.

C- Conventional morality.

D- Pre-operational stage.

72. A whole family sees a Social Worker. Upon learning about the family dynamics, he identifies the eldest child as the one that takes on all the responsibilities of the other family members. What role in the family theory system is the child playing?

A. Mascot.

B- Caretaker.

C- Identified Patient.

D- Victim.

73. A woman has been seeing a Clinical Social Worker for a period of one whole year. Over the year, she expressed an interest in losing weight. The SW has been talking to her about eating healthy food and exercising. Although the client wants to follow these methods, she eats fried chicken many times a week, other fast food and ice cream continuously. The SW tells her, "Ms. Jones, you've expressed an interest in dieting and say that you will try to use the methods I communicated to you. However, you continue to eat foods that are unhealthy. Do you see how that's contributing to your weight issue?" What technique is the SW using?

A. Reasoning.

B. Cognitive Behavioral Therapy.

C. Clarification.

D. Confrontation.

74. A teenager has recently learned that his mother is going to have a baby. After a few weeks, his parents notice that he has been wetting his bed. What likely defense mechanism is the teenager using?

A. Displacement.

B. Regression.

C. Manipulation.

D. Rapproachment.

75. A man has recently taken his ASWB exam. He did not prepare for the exam as much as he should have. When he missed the exam by 15 points, he said to himself,

"Well, the exam was difficult to begin with. It's not my fault. It's the people that wrote the exam." What defense mechanism is he using?

A. Rationalization.

B- Projection.

C Reaction Formation.

D Guilting.

76. A community Social Worker has recently observed that there is an increasing homelessness problem in a nearing neighborhood. She would like to get involved but knows that the homeless people will not know how to look for services. She contacts the Dept. of Homeless Services for assistance. What type of community practice is she using?

A. Social Reform.

B. Social Planning.

C. Social Action.

D. The Good Samaritan Act.

77. A male SW is researching the rate of the Diabetes epidemic in his neighborhood. He has learned that the rate has increased from 5% to 15% from last year. The SW wants

to partner with the community to try to alleviate this problem. What model of community organization is he using?

A. Social Planning.

B. Quantitative Data Analysis.

C. Social Reform.

D. Single-subject design.

78. A SW in an agency that assists clients with Intellectual Disabilities would like to test the adaptive skills of some of her clients. What testing method would be most appropriate?

A- MMPI.

B- WISC - R

C. Vineland Adaptive Scale.

D. Motivational Assessment Scale.

79. A woman sees an ER Social Worker. She reports that she recently experienced a huge stress and has been unable to see for a couple of days. What disorder is she likely suffering from?

A. Malingering.

B. Conversion Disorder.

C. Factitious Disorder.

D. Somatic Disorder.

80. A entire family is seen by a Social Worker. The mother reports that one of the 18-year-old daughters has just decided to leave home and move to another state. The mother states that there are a number of problems in the family and that this daughter's departure is a huge betrayal from the daughter towards the family. According to Bowenian Family Therapy, what process is being used in this instance?

A. Paradoxical Directive.

B. Emotional fusion.

C. Guilt.

D. Differentiation.

81. A 35-year-old man with Moderate Intellectual Disability was just found eating chalk from the garbage. The Direct Support Staff rush to his aid and see that he has started to eat chalk. What disorder is the man most likely suffering with?

A. Tic Disorder.

B. Tourette's Syndrome.

C. Tardive Dyskenesia.

D. PICA

82. A man is interested in conducting research on a new anti-depressant to test out its effectiveness on persons diagnosed with Persistent Depressive Disorder. After gathering the core group of subjects, what must the man do FIRST?

A- Administer the medication.

B- See if their families approve the experiment.

C- Have the subjects sign the consent form.

D- Develop a way to measure levels of depression after the administration of the medication.

83. A man has recently been diagnosed with Diabetes, Type II. His sugar level is somewhat high, and he needs help managing his condition. His doctor suggests a healthy lifestyle that includes diet and exercise, as well as medication. What type of Prevention strategy is the doctor using?

A- Cautious strategizing.

B- Secondary Prevention.

C- Tertiary Prevention.

D- Good common sense.

84. A woman has been experiencing a state of heightened emotions. She is unable to sleep for a couple of days, has thoughts of grandeur and goes on a spending spree with money that she has not earned yet. The entire period lasts for 4 days and then

the woman crashes. Her crashing includes not being able to get out of bed, not eating and a constant sad mood. What type of disorder is she likely displaying?

A- Mania.

B- Bipolar II Disorder.

C- Substance Abuse Withdrawal.

D- Bipolar I Disorder.

85. A young woman recently graduated from college. She has been employed at an entry-level job in a Social Services agency. The position requires her to attend weekly meetings with her colleagues. The woman rarely participates in these meetings. When asked to speak, she says very little. She goes home and tells her boyfriend that she is extremely afraid to be judged by her co-workers. What condition is she likely displaying?

A- Nervousness.

B- Acute Stress Disorder.

C- Social Anxiety Disorder.

D- Histrionic Personality Disorder.

86. A man is sitting in a Disability Office. He is being asked questions as to the state of his functional employability. The man answers the questions correctly. All of a sudden, he stares out the window and tells the Social Worker that "Someone out there is trying to get him." He also relays to the Social Worker that "Someone out there is out to get the Social Worker too. What disorder is the man most likely suffering with?

A- Schizophrenia.

B-. Grandiose Delusions

C-. Panic Disorder

D- Agoraphobia.

87. A teenager female is speaking with a Social Worker. She says that she cannot decide whether or not to stay with her boyfriend. She explains that she made a list of "Reasons to stay" and "Reasons to go." Some of the "Reasons to stay are" - He is a good provider; he is kind and loyal. Some of the "Reasons to leave are: " - He has a huge

temper. He is jealous and possessive of her and also tries to control her behavior. What type of Social Theory is reflective of this example?

A- Weighing the pros and cons.

B- Social Exchange Theory.

C- Role theory.

D- Social influence.

88. A male Social Worker sees a woman in a social services office. He moves close to the client but maintains proper physical boundaries. The woman is also wearing a head dress, although it's 100 degrees. All of a sudden. the client moves away from the SW in fear. The SW doesn't understand and asks if he did something wrong? What culture group does the woman most likely belong to?

A- Native American

B- Hispanic.

C- Arab- American.

D- Black American.

89. A man is invited to a case conference in an Orthodox Jewish social services organization. When he enters, he greets everyone and tries to shake hands with the female employees of the organization. The women move away and state that they do not shake hands. The man respects their requests. What type of social work value is the man displaying?

A- Respect to cultural differences.

B- Respect to women.

C- Politeness.

D- Cultural Diversity.

90. A woman comes in to see a Social Worker. She is convinced that because she had her children early and could not focus on getting her Social Work license, it is now too late. The sessions are centered around restructuring her thinking regarding her ability to get a license. The Social Worker asks the woman to write out her "Misery story" and reframe it into a "Success Story". What form of therapy is she using?

A- Positive Behavior Therapy.

B- Individual Therapy.

C- Narrative Therapy.

D- Cognitive-Behavioral Therapy.

91. A Direct Support Professional is working with a man with Severe Intellectual Disability.   He comes in for his shift and finds that there is a bruise on his clients' hip. He tells the Social Worker on the Unit that he observed a bruise on the clients' hip. He also notifies the SW that the client's bed does not have bed rails and he have a tendency to fall out of bed. What should the Social Worker do first?

A- Contact his superiors to obtain bed rails.

B - Fill out an Abuse Incident report and contact the proper authorities.

C- Refer the client to the doctor.

D- Monitor the bruise for a couple of days to see if it's still there.

92 - What does the DSM V stand for?

A- Diagnostic Sequential Manual of Mental Disorders. (Fifth edition)

B- Differential Statistician Manual. (Fifth edition).

C- Diagnostic Statistical Manual of Mental Disorders (fifth edition).

D- Disorders Statistical Manual (fifth edition.)

93 - A Social Worker accompanies her client to a psychiatric appointment. The psychiatrist recommends a medication regimen of Risperidone for disorganized thinking, elevated mood and also delusions of grandeur. What Disorder is the psychiatrist most likely treating?

A- Bipolar Disorder Type II

B- Schizophrenia

C- Depressive Disorder.

D- Bipolar I Disorder

94 -A Social Worker is working at a disability eligibility office. She is seeing a client and starts to explain to him that he may not be eligible for benefits. The client becomes

belligerent, starts yelling and cursing. Then, he proceeds telling the SW: "All you social workers are the same. You don't care about me; you just sit there and collect a paycheck." What should the social worker do first?

A- Call her supervisor.

B - Try to use validation techniques to calm the client down.

C- Call the authorities.

D- Ask the client to reschedule when he's feeling better.

95 - If a man asks the social worker to trade his "painting services" in exchange for social service sessions, what standard in the Code of Ethics does this fall under?

A- Inebriation.

B- Misrepresentation.

C- Dual relationships.

D- Conflict of Interests.

96 - A woman has a disagreement with her supervisor. The supervisor states that she must do a report one way and the woman suggests that she do it in a different way. The supervisor becomes upset and states that if she does not follow his guidelines, she will be terminated. According to French and Raven, what type of power is the supervisor using?

A- Expert Power.

B- Legitimate Power.

C- Coercive Power.

D- Abuse of Power.

97. A mother and her adult child come to the Social Work office for clinical services. The mother is the one that will be requiring the services. However, she does not speak any English and only speaks Urdu. Her son speaks English and asks if he could translate for her. What must the Social Worker do in this situation?

A- Agree to have the son translate.

B- Refer to another Social Worker.

C- Ask for a professional interpreter.

D- Suggest that a woman find a Social Worker who speaks Urdu.

98. A teenager has recently lost a loved one and wants to join a Bereavement group during the 3rd session. The group has already started, and the Group Leader has decided that the group will be closed-ended. The Group Co-Leader feels sorry for the man and asks the Group Leader to bend the rules. What must the Group leader do?

A- Allow the teenager to enter the group.

B- Explain to the teenager that the group has already started and refer him to a grief counselor.

C- Tell the teenager that he is unable to join the group despite the tragedy that occurred.

D- Ask the group members if they would mind if he joined the group.

99 - A woman goes to a restaurant. She is dressed in a very seductive fashion. She orders from the waiter but asks him questions every time he comes around. She is visibly upset when the waiter is not able to attend to her. What type of disorder is the woman likely suffering from?

A- Histrionic Personality Disorder.

B- narcissistic personality disorder.

C- borderline personality disorder.

D- Grandiose delusions.

100 - A man is seen at a clinic in a Social Worker's office. He reports that when he was a teenager, he was sexually abused. When asked about how he is feeling now, the man answers that he often has nightmares about the incident, relives the experience frequently and has trouble forming romantic relationships. What disorder is he likely suffering from?

A- Post traumatic stress disorder.

B- Trauma

C- Acute Stress Disorder.

D- Anti-social Personality disorder.

101- A young lady finds out that her cousin has cancer. She is extremely close to her cousin and is afraid of the cancer diagnosis. She proceeds by spending hours on the Internet to find out everything she possibly can about this condition. What defense mechanism is she likely using?

A- Projection

B- Sublimation

C- Denial

D- Intellectualization.

102 - A father brings in a son for an evaluation. He says that over the past day, the son has been exhibiting disorganized thoughts, has been saying there is a plot against him and has expressed false beliefs about his family members and loved ones. He is extremely concerned and says that this episode only happened today. Yesterday, the boy didn't exhibit any agitated thinking. What is the most likely diagnosis that the boy is exhibiting?

A- Schizophreniform.

B- Acute Stress Disorder.

C- Paranoid Schizohphrenia.

D - Brief Psychotic Disorder.

103- A man has reports to the Social Worker that he has an extreme need for excessive cleanliness. He always wears a mask when he is outside to protect himself from germs. He does not want to work in an office because he is afraid of being infected. He also washes his hands 100 times before he goes anywhere. What type of disorder is this most likely related to?

A- narcissistic personality disorder.

B- Impulse Control Disorder.

C- Social Anxiety Disorder.

D- obsessive compulsive disorder.

104 - A woman has been seen at a social work clinic for a period of 6 months. During the beginning of treatment, the woman spent 45 minutes of her session berating the Social Worker and saying how incompetent he is. However, when the session was almost over, she proceeded to prolong the session by coming up with an extremely personal traumatic situation. During treatment, she also reported poor attachment styles and extremely complicated and dramatic relationships. What disorder is this reminiscent of?

A- narcissistic personality disorder.

B- borderline personality disorder.

C- Manipulative Disorder.

D- Intrusive conversion disorder.

105 - A woman brings her daughter into treatment with a Social Worker. The child is 7 years old. The woman states that her daughter becomes very irritable when plans are changed. She also refuses to do anything that is asked of her. She becomes extremely uncomfortable when she is not involved in activities. What disorder is she most likely displaying?

A- Conduct Disorder.

B- Anti Social Personality Disorder.

C- Oppositional Defiant Disorder.

D- Normal development for that age group.

106 - What is the most likely treatment choice for ADHD?

A - Paxil.

B - Adderal.

C - Trazadone.

D- Acetomenaphine.

107 - What medication is most likely used for depression and insomnia?

A- Ambien.

B- Trazadone.

C- Valium.

D- Wellbutrin.

108 - A 15-year-old girl and her family come in to see a Social Worker. The mother declares in a very emotional way that her daughter just became pregnant. The family is very religious in nature and respect and observe religious laws. The mother discloses to the SW that her daughter wants to terminate the pregnancy, despite religious teachings.

The mother is adamant that the baby is born and that they will find a way to deal with the situation later. The daughter states: "It is my life and I have decided not to keep this baby". What should the SW do?

A- Convince the mother that she should go along with the abortion decision.

B- Encourage the daughter to keep the baby.

C- Normalize the daughter's feelings and state that "she has a right to her own decision.

D- Suggest family therapy for the family.

109 - A Persian woman and her daughter come in for Social Work Services. The daughter is 17 years old and states that she has occasional heavy periods and discomfort with her private parts. The PCP suggested that the young woman is examined by a gynecologist. The mother states that according to Persian law, the woman must remain a virgin until her wedding night. She worries that the daughter will lose her virginity if examined by a gynecologist. The daughter is not insistent on being examined, based upon the law. What should the Social Worker do first?

A- Insist that the girl is examined by a gynecologist to prevent damage.

B- Respect the mother's and daughter's wishes and continue to work with them.

C- Contact Child Protective Services in order to safeguard the child from medical neglect.

D- Call the Primary Care Physician and ask them to convince them to seek gynecological services.

110 - What medication regimen would a psychiatrist likely to prescribe for Persistent Depressive Disorder?

A- Geodon.

B- Invega

C- Prozac.

D- Buspar.

111- A social worker observes a client with Intellectual Disabilities hitting his own head repeatedly? What should be the first source of Assessment for this client?

A - Behavior Modification

B- Referral to a physician.

C- Calming techniques.

D- Send the client to his room.

112- A woman comes into session. She is walking with an unsteady gait, is slurring her words and has alcohol on her breath? What should the SW do FIRST?

A- Send her away.

B- Ask if she can call a family member or a friend to pick her up.

C- Treat her.

D- Suggest an A.A. meeting.

113- What is the purpose of the Interdisciplinary Team?

A- To discuss perspectives.

B- To come to a consensus regarding the client.

C- To air out differences.

D- To argue until they come to an agreement.

114 - A Group SW Leader gets a job offer to move to another city. She needs to leave in a month. What should the SW do FIRST?

A- Inform her supervisor that she needs to leave and allow the Supervisor to take over.

B- Look for a replacement Group Leader to take her place.

C- Terminate the group immediately.

D- Notify the Board of Directors in her agency that she is leaving.

115. A Clinical Social Worker sees an individual for private session for a period of 3 months. They have formed a good therapeutic alliance. The client says she really likes the SW and would like to recommend her husband to the Clinical SW. How should the SW react?

A- Thank the client.

B- Accept the referral.

C- Explain to the client that accepting her husband as a client is not ethical and refer him to another SW.

D- Suggest couples counseling with the couple.

116 - A client is seen by a SW in a private clinic Unexpectedly, the client becomes very upset and says: "I need to see what you're writing about me. Let me see your notes." What should the SW do NEXT?

A- Hand Over the Notes.

B- Argue with the client.

C- Tell him it's not permissible.

D- Allow him to see just enough for him to be satisfied.

117 - A Clinical SW is scheduled to see a client for an hour. After 30 minutes, she notices a text from her family member that there is an emergency. She apologizes to the client and tells the client that she needs to go home. After she returns back after a week, she records in her progress notes that she saw the client for 1 hour. What standard in the Code of Ethics is she violating?

A- Competence.

B- Conflicts of Interest.

C- Billing.

D- Client Transfer.

118- A SW is conducting an observation of a facility with clients with Mild Intellectual l Disabilities. One man runs up and wants to hug the social worker. What should the Social Worker do?

A- Offer to shake hands instead.

B - Hug the client.

C- Tell the client that it is inappropriate and refuse the hug.

D- Leave the client and go to a different area.

119 - A man has hostility towards his father. During one of the sessions, the Social Worker suggests that he attempts the "Empty Chair technique" in order to express himself to his father. What type of therapy model is this consistent with?

A- Jungian Therapy.

B- Gestalt Therapy.

C- Cognitive-behavioral approach.

D- Psychoanalysis.

120 - A research SW wants to conduct an experiment, in which she will test out a new medication, said to be effective for symptoms of OCD. The group that will receive the medication is called.

A- Control group

B- Stratified group.

C- Experimental group.

D- Sample group.

121 - Michelle Obama is planning to develop a Diabetes Awareness training in her local community. What should Michelle do FIRST?

A- Garner support from the council representatives.

B- Distribute flyers and e-mails to invite people to the Training.

C- Ask political leaders to come to the training to offer their support.

D- Gauge the interest of the community to attend this type of training.

122 - "Randall Pearson" (on the This is Us show) has been informed that the tenants in his building are having problems with heat. Randall is no longer the building owner but holds a Social Work position. The landlords and tenants are fighting over this issue. Randall is asked to help them arrive at a solution. What is Randall's function.

A- The negotiator.

B- The mediator.

C- Change Agent.

D- Community Representative.

123 - There is state-wide policy on Public Assistance reform in the state of Florida. Many individuals who are in need of assistance are being denied benefits. The SW steps in to help solve the problem. What type of advocacy is the Social Worker conducting?

A- Macro Level Advocacy.

B- Change Advocacy.

C- Reform.

D- Fair Hearing Advocacy Development.

124 - A Social Worker notices that there is an increase in the homeless population in their community. The Social Worker takes initiative and begins speaking to the population about popular options. Upon conversations with the homeless population, he notices that they are not capable for advocating for themselves. He partners up with the local social services community group to offer his help. What Community model is the Social Worker using?

A- Social Planning.

B- Social Action.

C- Social Reform.

D- Social Change.

125 - A college professor would like to test the effectiveness of her college materials to assess the knowledge base of her students across time? What kind of research design would she use?

A- Cross-Sectional Study.

B- Longitudinal Study.

C- Quasi-Experimental Design.

D- Pre-affiliation design.

126. A SW is treating a young man with a history of suicidal thoughts and attempts. During the last 6 month-period, the man has been coming in feeling very unmotivated and lethargic. However, in the last few sessions, the man has revealed that he has been having increased energy, more motivation and an overall better sense of well-being. What should the SW assume may be happening?

A- The treatment worked.

B- The man no longer has suicidal thoughts.

C- The increased energy could indicate that he could have more strength now to go through with the suicide.

D- He has stopped planning means of killing himself.

127 - A group is in its development stage and are getting to know one another. During the group process, all the questions and comments are being directed to the Group Leader? What stage of the group process is the group likely to be in?

A- Pre-affiliation.

B- Intimacy stage.

C- Cohesion.

D- Termination.

128 - A Social Worker is evaluating the data collection of her clients' target behaviors of the past 3 months. What type of research is being done?

A- Qualitative research.

B- Quantitative research.

C- Frequency distribution.

D- Data Analysis.

129 - A Social Work tutor wants to assess her students' progress with her lessons. She uses an Assessment phase in her tutoring, followed by the tutoring sessions themselves and the post-test to measure the students' progress. What type of design is she using?

A- Chi square.

B- Anova.

C- AB design.

D - ABAB design.

130 - During data collection of clients' target behavior, the SW notices that the number 10 (relating to 10 behaviors) appears most often. What is that number called in a graph distribution?

A - The meridian.

B- The median.

C- The mode.

D- The Chi Square.

131 - "Amy Farrah Fowler" (From the Big Bang Theory) is selecting subjects for her experiment on human behavior. She selects only the group of people that are residing in Santa Monica CA. What type of process is she using?

A- Stratified sampling.

B- Group sampling.

C- Simple Random Sampling.

D- Quasi-Experimental Design.

132 - A community is gathered in a church and are deciding how to allocate funds to the Annual Christmas social event. What type of community theory is this an example of?

A- Conflict theory.

B- Power and Control.

C- Power struggle.

D- Hostility Model.

133 - What technique is associated with Person-Centered therapy?

A - Person centered technique.

B- Self-Actualizing tendency.

C- Unconditional positive regard.

D- Acceptance.

134 - A parent disciples their children by using clear boundaries, however, discusses the consequences of their actions with them and seeks conversation. What type of parenting style is she using?

A- Permissive style.

B- Authoritative

C- Authoritarian.

D- Diplomatic style.

135 - A man in a Social Worker's office tells the Social Worker that he believes the French culture is superior to others. What is that phenomenon called?

A- Cultural Superiority.

B- Cultural Diversity.

C- Ethnocentrism.

D- Ignorance.

136- A woman is seen in her home by a Social Worker because she is extremely fearful of crowds. She tells the Social Worker she has not left her home in years, even to attend her daughter's wedding. What type of disorder is the woman likely suffering from?

A - Social Anxiety Disorder.

B- Anxious Disorder.

C- Avoidant Personality Disorder.

D- Agoraphobia.

137- A family is seen for therapy. During the course of the conversation, the Social Worker notices that the father in the family is consistently dismissing all the problems by joking about them. What is his most likely role in the family?

A- Class clown.

B- Mascot.

C- Supporter.

D- Hero.

138 - A native American boy runs away from the reservation to the nearby town. While he is in town, he discloses that he has serious issues with his family, and he does not receive support from his parents or grandparents. A social worker assists the boy in coming back to the reservation. When he finds the boy's parents, he says, 'Please let me help the boy with some of the issues he's been having." However, the father says that the tribe will take care of the boys' needs. What social Act is the father adhering to?

A- The Education of All Handicapped Children Act of 1975.

B- HIPAA

C- ADA

D- The Indian Children Welfare Act of 1978.

139 - A man comes to see a Social Worker for several conditions. He states that he believes one of his primary problems is that he is very socially isolated and needs extended periods of time to be by himself. The client says that he is not sure what that situation is all about. What is the best test of measurement for the Social Work to use to help the client?

A- A Personality Exam

B- Myers Briggs.

C- MMPI.

D- Beck Depression Inventory.

140 - A Social Worker notices that there is a client in the waiting room that she has had a former relationship with. They exchange a friendly hello, and the man comes up to the SW and asks if she would be willing to offer him her SW services? The woman agrees. What standard in the Code of Ethics is the SW violating?

A- Sexual interests.

B- Conflict of interests.

C- Social Relationships.

D- Dual relationships.

141 - A secretary in a Social Worker's office is talking loudly to her colleague. The conversation has to do with one of the clients that is being treated in the SW's office. What standard in the Code of Ethics is being violated?

A- Confidentiality.

B- Privacy and Confidentiality.

C- HIPAA

D- Respect.

142 - A client sends her Social Worker a Facebook request. What should the Social Worker do?

A- Accept the request.

B- Deny the request and explain to the client that it is not considered ethical practice for her to engage in an extraneous relationship with the client, outside of treatment.

C- Delete her Facebook account.

D- Refer her to another Social Worker.

143 - A social worker works in a rural area and her clients are often limited in financial resources. One of her clients asks for services in an exchange for chickens from her farm. What should the Social Worker do?

A- Tell her it's unacceptable.

B- Agree to the trade.

C- Agree to the trade, only with the client's Informed consent to acquiesce to such an arrangement.

D- Do nothing.

144- A man with Intellectual Disabilities is prescribed an anti-psychotic medication. The man can't advocate for himself or make an informed decision. However, this medication is necessary for his treatment and his progress. How should the consent be obtained?

A- The man should put an "X" next to the signature line.

B- The agency should act as his representative.

C- An aunt, who is not a legal guardian should sign.

D- A legal community representative who agreed to make decisions on his behalf, should sign.

145 - A client asks her Social Worker if she can recommend an anti-anxiety medication? What should the SW do?

A- Refer her to a psychiatrist.

B- Recommend a medication that worked for others before.

C- Tell her she does not know of any anti-anxiety medications.

D- Deflect the question.

146. - A rock star has recently been treated for substance addiction. She has been withdrawing from the addiction and has been experiencing restless and bone pain. What substance was she most likely using?

A- Heroin.

B- Alcohol.

C- Cocaine.

D- Marijuana.

147. - Using the question above, what is the most likely treatment choice for this rock stars' addiction?

A- Antabuse.

B- Suboxone.

C- Medication.

D- Coffee.

148.- A client came to a Social Worker for assistance. During the interview, he discloses that he has had suicidal thoughts. After completing the Suicide Risk Assessment, the Social Worker finds that the man has the plan, means and time set for executing the suicide what should the Social Worker do NEXT?

A- Talk him out of the plan.

B- Recommend more individual and group therapy.

C- Ask him if he can call the Psychiatric ER for him.

D- Continue to ask him more questions regarding his suicidal ideation and plan.

149. - A 15-year-old girl has recently found out that she's pregnant. She is terrified but insists that she is set on keeping the baby. She has not discussed the situation with her parents or her boyfriend. The social worker thinks that it is best for the girl to discuss the situation with her loved ones. What should the SW do FIRST?

A- Tell the girl that she's obligated to tell her family.

B- Respect her right not to inform her loved ones about the pregnancy.

C- Encourage her to consult her parents.

D- Insist that she is too young to undertake this pregnancy.

150.- A man just told his SW that recently he has been diagnosed with cancer. The man insists that traditional medical practices are dangerous and believes in alternative treatment. He tells the SW that although his oncologist recommended chemotherapy, he is going to go to a natural healer for alternative healing methods. What should the SW do NEXT?

A- Tell the man that the healer may not be certified in medicine and therefore should not be trusted.

B- Tell the man that alternative methods are a bad idea.

C- Ask him to think about the situation more carefully.

D- Respect his choice to proceed with alternative treatments.

151. - A woman has recently started social work services for symptoms of depression. After meeting with this woman, establishing rapport and providing a full assessment, what should the Social Worker do NEXT?

A- Discuss and plan a treatment with the client.

B- Engage the client in supportive psychotherapy.

C- Ask her to consider visiting a psychiatrist.

D- Start working on goals to help her treat her depression.

152.- A hospital social worker is servicing a man who has been admitted to the hospital for a stroke. What should the Social Worker be thinking of in terms of a discharge plan?

A- Linkages to other hospitals.

B- Assistive devices, such as crutches, home health care and outpatient services.

C- Continued supportive psychotherapy.

D- Emphasis on collateral participation.

153- For the above question, when should termination process begin for this client?

A- After the client is discharged.

B- A Day before the client is discharged.

C- A month in advance.

D- As soon as the man is admitted.

154.- A SW employed in an administrative capacity has a problem with retaining staff. Staff are suffering from severe burn-out and attendance is at an all-time low. What should the Administrator do?

A- Boost staff morale by enacting an "Employee of the Month" program.

B- Changing the "sick leave" policy to make it more stringent.

C- Hire more employees.

D- Change the overall policies prescribed by the agency regarding benefits, employee recognition and wages.

155 - In Macro development, what is the role of the Initiator?

A- He is the person that is first to recognize a problem.

B- He is the individual that initiates the process.

C- He is the individual that handles hostility and manages conflicts.

D- He is the individual that advocates for the policy.

156 - A young woman came into a social worker's office to discuss her situation following a recent breakup. She stated that she was with her boyfriend for a long time, and she feels lost without him. She discloses that she does not know if she can cope with this terrible loss. What should a social worker do FIRST?

A- Refer her to a support group.

B- Explore her feelings about the relationship.

C- Complete a suicide risk assessment.

D- Suggest couples counseling.

157- What is one of the reasons an interagency conflict can exist?

A- Competition for resources.

B- A difference of opinion across the multiple domains in an agency.

C- Personality Clashes

D- Personnel Burnout

158- Why should the Human Resources Department complete job analyses?

A- To monitor staff performance.

B- To create different opportunities.

C- To develop job descriptions.

D- To explain job duties to personnel.

159 - What is an example of a Collective Action to get a social policy to be accepted?

A- To form a task force.

B- To collaborate on the processes for the change effort.

C- To raise awareness regarding an issue.

D - Organizing a boycott to bring about salary increases.

160 - A man comes in to discuss his recent job loss. He says that he has been traumatized by the decision to terminate his position. He tells the SW that he has been reliving the experience repeatedly, experiencing nightmares and having a general state of unease. What is the first way a Social Worker can help him?

A- Refer him to a medical professional.

B- Acknowledge his feelings of loss and devastation.

C- Discuss job opportunities with him.

D- Inquire about his financial resources to ensure he has adequate support.

161 - A Social Worker discloses to her Social Work Supervisor that she has been having personal problems that have been impeding her work at the clinic. What should the Social Work Supervisor do?

A- Encourage her to take some "time off" to cope with her problems and come back when she's feeling better.

B- Offer her individual therapy.

C- Explain to her that she cannot continue to work there.

D- Re-arrange her caseload.

162 - An interdisciplinary Team is meeting to discuss a medication recommendation by a psychiatrist. The Team is not in agreement with the medication choice and do not want to administer it to the client. What should the IDT do?

A- Proceed with the Psychiatrist's recommendation, as written.

B- Involve the client's parents.

C- Invite the Psychiatrist into the Meeting to discuss treatment options.

D- Refuse to take the Psychiatrist's recommendation.

163. A School Social Worker is called in to a meeting to discuss behavior problems that a student has been having   the mother of the student is also present. At one point, the mother requests to see the client's chart. When she reviews the chart, she disagrees with some of the information that has been written about her daughter. What should the SW do?

A- Refuse to change the information.

B- Ask the mother why it is so important for her to have the information recorded as she sees fit.

C- Involve the principal into the discussion.

D- Invite the mother to change the information, as she has the right to alter the information in her child's record.

164 - A - A transgender male seeks the help of a Social Worker because he believes he has not been able to get a job due to the nature of his gender identity. The SW should FIRST:

A- Offer understanding.
B- Help him to fight the organization that refused him employment.
C- Encourage him to look for a job somewhere else.
D- Ask him about other means of financial support.

165 - An Intellectually Disabled woman has become pregnant by a fellow resident. Neither of them is sexually consenting. The IDT is discussing strategies of action for this client. How should the Interdisciplinary Team proceed?

A- Help the woman proceed with the pregnancy.
B- Ask a family member of legal guardian to advocate on her behalf.
C- Assist the woman in scheduling an abortion.
D- Seek the counsel of a Mental Health legal attorney.

166 - A social worker in an Administrative Capacity wants to refer a family friend for placement in residential services. The woman is not the right fit for this particular program. The Administrator is also aware that the residential facility needs to fill a bed in order to bill for Medicaid. What the SW do?

A- Refer her anyway.

B- Seek alternative arrangements for the woman that fits her needs.

C- Hold a meeting with her colleagues to discuss the situation.

D- Tell the family that she is unable to help them.

167 - Land developers want to tear down a homeless shelter in order to build an income-increasing co-op. This would mean that hundreds of homeless people would have nowhere to go. What is the best strategy for the Community to retain the shelter?

A- Go to City Hall to fight the issue.

B- Hold a Community Forum to discuss the situation.

C- Hold a fund-raising event and invite the land developers to attend.

D- Argue with the landowners until there is a resolution.

168 - Members of a community don't like seeing the Intellectually Disabled client population walking around the neighborhood. What is the best strategy to help the neighbors to accept this particular client population into their neighborhood?

A- To speak to the community members on the street.

B- To hold a "Block party" next to the residential facility where the Intellectually Disabled clients reside.

C- To write letters to the local councilman.

D- To organize a meeting to protest the community.

169- A social work tutor wants to see if there is a correlation between her sessions and the students achieving a passing score on the exam. She thinks that there is a positive relationship between those 2 variables. She is starting a Research design to test this hypothesis. What should the SW do in the beginning of the study?

A- Accept the null hypothesis.

B- Reject the null hypothesis.

C- Perform an ANOVA analysis.

D- Conduct the experiment.

170- A community is opposed to having a group home in their neighborhood with individuals who have Down's Syndrome and Autistic Spectrum Disorder. What should the social services agency do?

A- Buy the house anyway.

B- Tell them "It's a free country."

C- Invite the community members to a meeting to provide psychoeducation on these particular client populations.

D - Look for a house in a more accepting neighborhood.

171 A community social worker attends a board meeting and proposes a suggestion for sanitation improvement in the neighborhood. The community members don't like this suggestion and relay that they could really benefit from having an after-school program in their neighborhood. What should the Social Worker do NEXT?

A- Create a task force to help with the sanitation project.

B- Invite the stakeholders to contribute to the project.

C- Gauge the interests of the community regarding the implications of sanitation concern.

D- Start a Facebook campaign to attract more attention to the sanitation issue.

172 - A Social Work Supervisor gets a complaint from one of the supervisees regarding another one of his team members. What should the SW supervisor do NEXT?

A- Invite both supervisees in for a meeting.

B- Seek opinions from the remaining staffs.

C- Redirect the complaint back to the original complainant and offer strategies on how to best deal with the problem.

D- Address the issue during the next staff meeting.

173- A child is referred to a School Social Worker by his teacher for issues of truancy and lack of concentration during class. The student comes in a for couple of sessions, with no results. Prior to this incident, there were no academic or behavioral issues with this student. What should the School Social Worker do NEXT?

A- Speak to the teacher more about the situation.

B- Contact the parents and invite them in for a meeting.

C- Call Child Protective Services.

D- Refer the child for a psychological evaluation.

174- A 16-year-old girls to a Social Worker regarding problems with her boyfriend. There are indications that the girl is having sex with the boyfriend. What should the Social Worker do first?

A- Continue listening to the girl.

B- Consult state legislation on matters of "statutory rape".

C- Tell the girl that she cannot listen to any more information on this matter.

D- Contact the girl's parents.

175 - A woman tells a social worker that she is extremely annoyed with her sister and wants to do away with her. What is the BEST thing for the SW to do?

A- Remind her of the limits of confidentiality

B- Warn the sister.

C- Clarify what the woman means by "Do away with?"

D- Continue the session, as scheduled.

176 - A man comes in for an initial session. He complains of mood changes, rapid weight loss and confusion/ What should the Social Worker do FIRST?

A- Assess the severity of the mood swings.

B- Get more information from collateral sources.

C- Do a complete chart review.

D- Refer the man to a physician.

177- A young woman starts sessions with a Social Worker. She states she has multiple problems with prior social workers and just knows that this time, it will be different.

What should the SW do FIRST?

A- Tell the woman, "Thank you".

B- Clarify the expectations of the social worker/client relationship.

C- Build the therapeutic alliance between them.

D- Proceed with the Assessment process.

178 - A client's aunt calls the Social Worker on the phone. She would like to discuss her niece's progress in therapy. What should the SW do FIRST?

A- Tell her that she needs to schedule a family session.

B- Inform her that you she cannot discuss any client information with her.

C- Tell the aunt about the niece's progress in therapy.

D- Terminate with the client.

179- An elderly client is scheduled for an Intake session. During the session, she does not focus on topic and redirect the conversation to memories regarding her family.

What should the Social Worker do FIRST?

A- Allow her to continue reminiscing.

B- Re-orient the client back to topic.

C- Schedule another appointment.

D- Ask her questions in between her discussing her memories.

180 - A client is mandated to come in for treatment post-incarceration. He is angry and states that he does not want to be there. What should the SW do?

A- Remind the client that he needs to participate in the session.

B- Tell him that she needs to report his resistance to his parole officer.

C- Validate his resistance and ask him more questions about having to be in therapy.

D- Refer him to another Social Worker?

181 - The same client as in question 185 has not shown up for one of his sessions.

What should the SW do?

A- Leaving a message on his cell phone.

B- Write a note on his case record.

C- Contact his parole officer.

D- Schedule another session.

182 - A client comes in for symptoms of depression. What is one testing instrument that a Social Worker can use to assess him?

A- MMPI

B- The Beck Depression Inventory Scale.

C- Thematic Apperception Test.

D- Rorscharch Inkblot Test.

183 - A client with Schizophrenia becomes angry during a session. He proceeds to raise his hand and attempt to hit the Social Worker? What should the Social Worker do?

A- Help the client to calm down.

B- Ask the client to sit down.

C- Use other calming techniques.

D- Escape the situation.

184 - A social worker has been sued by a client. There is information in his progress notes that could help him with the lawsuit. What should the Social Worker do?

A- Resist using the notes, as it is a breach of confidentiality.

B- Use a portion of the notes, as dictated by the Code of Ethics.

C- Use the necessary notes in order to defend himself.

D- Ask the legal representative for clarification.

185 -A client has been seeing a social worker for a period of 2 years. Recently, she has disclosed to the Social Worker that she is moving. She would like to continue with the Social Worker via Tele-therapy. After checking with state legislation about this type of treatment, the SW learns that it's acceptable to continue on in this fashion. What should the Social Worker do NEXT?

A- Happily accept the request.

B- Speak to her supervisor.

C- Remind the client of the risks associated with Tele-therapy.

D- Tell the client she cannot accommodate her.

186 - A division in an agency has been experiencing budget cuts. What is the BEST action an Administrator can undertake in this situation.?

A- Reduce employees' wages.

B- Eliminate the client's music program.

C- Limit the number of holiday party in the division.

D- Do away with bonuses for the coming year.

187- What is the best way to evaluate a program?

A- Do a complete historical review.

B- Ask administrative staff for assistance.

C- Do an external audit.

D- Ask line staff for information.

188 - The client comes in due to problems at work, sleeping problems and extreme mood shifts. He also reports an increase in alcohol use. What is the first thing a Social Worker should do?

A- Refer the client for a physical evaluation.

B- Inquire more into the increase in alcohol use.

C- Perform a mental status exam.

D- Arrange for a psychiatric evaluation for the client.

189- A man vacillates between having excessive lethargy and an excess in energy for the last 2 years. What is the most likely diagnosis?

A- Bipolar I Disorder.

B- Bipolar II Disorder.

C- Cyclothymia.

D- Depressive Disorder NOS.

190- A young man would like to form relationships but is afraid of rejection. What is the most likely diagnosis?

A- Schizotypal Personality Disorder.

B- Anti-social Personality Disorder.

C- Schizoaffective Personality Disorder.

D- Avoidant Personality Disorder.

191- A woman's friend shares some disturbing news with her about her medical condition. She discusses the condition in great detail. However, 2 months later, when the friend brings up her medical condition, the woman cannot recall the important details about the situation. What defense mechanism does this reflect?

A- Displacement

B- Repression

C- Sublimation

D- Forgetting

192 - A woman in a hospital has been deemed as brain-dead. The physician states that there will be no improvement in her condition. However, her family doesn't want her taken off life support. They consult with the Social Worker regarding their options. What should a Social Worker do NEXT?

A- Help them understand the validity of the medical advice.

B- Support them in the decision to keep the woman on life support.

C- Explore Advanced Directives prescribed by the woman.

D- Encourage the family to talk to their spiritual advisor.

193 - A Social Worker is seeing a client from a different culture. What must she do to understand the client better?

A- Gather information from colleagues about this particular culture group.

B- Transfer the client to a Social Worker that is of the same culture.

C- Inquire about the client's culture through direct communication.

D- Attend a cultural event with her.

194 - A team of social workers in a senior citizens center has been working on a project. They wish to improve the recreational program for the elderly. Once the project is finalized, the Team leader brings the finished plan to the supervisor. The supervisor is pleased and tells the leader that he did a great job. How should the team leader respond?

A- Accept the compliment and tell him "Thank you".

B- Show him other ideas that he has for an upcoming project.

C- Bring up the possibility for a promotion.

D- Tell him the current project was a team effort.

195 - What stage in the Tuckman Model of Group development corresponds to the stage of "Power in Control" in the Boston Model of Group formation?

A - Storming

B- Performing

C- Norming

D- Forming.

196 - What is the best definition of the concept of Accommodation?

A- Modifying new information to fit into our schemas.

B- Modifying our schemas to accommodate new information.

C- Pleasing others.

D- Being compliant with others.

197 - What is the best predictor that sexual abuse occurred in the below-mentioned minor?

A- The Adolescent fondled another teen

B- A teen who is dressed in a provocative manner

C- Excessive masturbation.

D- The teen covers up excessively

198 - Statistically, which population group is "at most-risk for suicide"

A- Arab Americans.

B- Black American Women.

C- Older White Males.

D- Adolescents

199- A Social Worker instituted a program for "Immigration adjustment" in a culturally diverse neighborhood. Even though, she advertised the service heavily and informed existing clients, the community members haven't showed up to meetings. What should the SW do FIRST?

A- Close down the program.

B- Move the program to another location.

C- Ask the community members about their preferences for days and times.

D- Speak to her supervisor.

200 - What is the best treatment source for opiod addiction?

A- Benzodiazepines.

B- Vivitrol

C- Paxil

D- Allegra

(**Note**: Some questions were repeated, so I am adding these additional questions.)

201 - A SW's client is on trial for attempted murder. The Social Worker is court ordered to present her process recordings to be used for the trial. What should the SW do?

A- Present the information; however, request that it is protected from public records and is under seal.

B- Present the information with no limitations.

C- Stand on confidentiality.

D- Challenge the court.

202- What medication is used to take away side effects of anti-psychotic medication?

A- Risperidone

B- Abilify

C- C- Eskalith

D- Cogentin

203- What diagnosis is characterized by involuntary jerky movements and a protruding tongue?

A- Tic Disorder

B- Anxiety Disorder

C- Tardive Dyskenesia.

D- Panic Syndrome.

204- In research, what is considered the mid-point on the graph?

A- Mode

B- Median

C- Mean

D- Average

CONTENT

Just like Forest Gump said, "Life is like a box of chocolates, you never know what you're going to get". This applies to the ASWB exam, as well. You never know which types of questions you will get, so study everything. You don't need to memorize every single thing, but as long as you know concepts associated with a theory/therapy, you will be ok. I will explain later what content is more important to know and what content is less of a priority.

Special Note: The Content and Sections in the Exam are divided into Direct Practice and Indirect Practice.

Direct Practice: involves practice with a client, group, couple or family.

Indirect Practice: refers more to partnering with the community; becoming involved with social policy or procedure in order to change it.

Chapter 5

Development: (Human Development in the Social Environment.)

You may be asking yourself why, as a Social Worker you need to study development. The reason is to understand a client/patient, in terms of their functioning at the time.

All human beings go through a process of development/maturation. We all go through the progression of meeting developmental milestones, such as "turning over", crawling, pulling up to standing, walking, etc. In the case of Intellectual Disabilities (formerly Mental Retardation); individuals do not develop at a normal rate. For example, they may never develop speech, walking, toilet training or may be arrested in different stages of development. However, in the case of "regular" individuals, development is part and parcel of their progress.

Development and the Life Cycle:

Development affects an individual's way, as to his/her self-esteem, life cycle, etc. It is also particularly pertinent to the different age groups. For example, in the elderly population, this may manifest itself in a lack of meaning or purpose in life. Since senior citizens may stop "being productive members of society", they may feel as if they are worthless and useless. Also, if their children move away or they lose friends, this will enhance a sense of isolation/loneliness. Part of our tasks are to encourage them to talk about past life events with them and also to create meaningful opportunities for them.

In the **adolescence life stage**, teenagers go through a period of "storm and stress". They experience physiological and emotional changes, which cause them to alter the way they perceive their reality. Additionally, they experience turbulence in their social roles, family roles and personality changes. It is a challenging time in their lives, and we must be sensitive to their sudden shifts in persona.

Examining the developmental life stages is crucial to the exam, since we must include varying techniques in our treatment of different age groups.

That being said, the theorists all formulated their own hypotheses of how individuals develop. Some theorists have a viewpoint of how each person is affected based on the resolution/lack of resolution of a stage of development.

Erikson postulated the Social Theory of Development. He believed that development continues throughout the lifespan. **Piaget** developed "the theory of learning of forming concepts". As the infant is born, the world around him is strange and he does not understand anything around him. Through the process of <u>cognitive development</u>, the formation of concepts/learning now to think, the individual is able to grow and understand the world. Some of Freud's beliefs are based on the theory of his psychosexual stages. He felt that each stage is formed by a pleasure principle attached to it. Mahler contribution of the theory of development is object relationships. This is the theory which, according to Mahler affects interpersonal functioning. You can think of Mahler's theory as boundary formation/ a steppingstone to attachment theory. She believes that depending on how the individual passes the stages, he/she will have healthy or unhealthy attachments to others. Kohlberg believed in the theory of moral development/ the theory of "right and wrong". He believed that true morality is never fully developed. However, we go through stages to arrive at a state of moral behavior.

Having said that, we will dive into the 5 main theorists that you need to know for the exam.

Chapter 6

Main Theorists:

Approximately 27 % of the exam covers Human theory and development, so let's get those theorists out of the way! :)

Social Development:

Since we are in the arena of social work, the most crucial theorist will be Erik Erikson. Erikson presents a theory of Social Development as delineated by stages that the individual in question must complete. This allows the person to advance to the next productive phase of Social Development. *One of the differences between Erikson and other theorists is that his theory covers the entire lifespan, while others may only go up to adolescence and etc.*

According to Erikson, the successful or unsuccessful resolution of these stages will have an impact on the subject's later social evolution. The stages occur throughout the entire life span and are marked by age groups that accompanies each stage.

As there are 8 stages and there are 4 stages that start with the "I" initial, it can get confusing, so I developed mnemonics (memory tricks) to help remember the stages more easily.

How this translates itself over to the exam: If the theory scenario on the question describes a social development situation, it will most likely be Erikson. Social development can be thought of as a way of relating to others.

Erikson's Bio-Psychosocial Stages of Development: Key Points: This personality theory lasts throughout the lifespan; Resolved vs. Unresolved Stages; The names of the stages will have something to do with the evolvement of the stage; Ages are crucial as they are a clue into what's happening at that life stage **A useful technique is to remember the name of the stage. For ex. Trust - has to do with an infant achieving trust in the world; Distrust occurs when an infant does not feel safety/trust in the world; Therefore, it is Trust vs. Mistrust.**

1- Trust vs Mistrust (Birth to 1 ½ years);   When the baby is born, the most important need is a sense of safety, which should be provided by the caretaker; Resolved stage: results in a sense of Trust in self and others; Unresolved : results in Mistrust (if the infant is not nurtured or taken care of) – (Studies showed that babies who were not hugged grew up with severe pathologies)

2- Autonomy vs. Shame Vs. Doubt (1 ½ - 3 years); (Fine and gross motor skills are being developed); Fine motor skills – ability to pick up objects using fingers: Gross Motor skills - using larger body muscles; grasping; moving standing up, using arm and leg coordination. Autonomy also arises out of a sense of social connection with parents.

At approximately age 2 – speech begins developing

(The mastery and achievement of motor and communication skills results in a sense of accomplishment/independence – Independence is synonymous with Autonomy; thus, the resolution of this stage is a sense of Autonomy; Unresolved: The child feels ashamed because they can't achieve, they skills and thus start to doubt themselves

3 - Initiative Vs. Guilt (3 – 6 years old) ; the child branches out into more open and public places; has a natural sense of curiosity/exploration; if Resolved: If the child is allowed to explore, they achieve a sense of initiative, which translates into later life; If Unresolved: they   become   fearful   and   guilty   –   the   opposite   of initiative./withdrawn/laid   back.   Initiative - taking charge; Guilt: - staying back/becoming more passive/withdrawn.

4. Industry vs. Inferiority (7-11 yrs. Old/ like the store.); At this age group,   the   child starts becoming judged on school performance; The child breaks out of   the "bubble" of life at home and learn how to adhere to a routine schedule.

   Think of school as their industry at that time period; if Resolved: it   results in a   sense of Mastery of Tasks (a sense of being productive/industrial); If Unresolved: will   start to feel inferior as compared toothier peer group.

5.   Identity   vs.   Identity   Diffusion/Role   Confusion   12-   18   years   old;   During adolescence, the individual is trying to figure who she/he is in the sense of identity. In   the process, he/she may try different roles for size (ex. Dressing up like Madonna or Lady   Gaga, depending on your generation ☉); If resolved: A sense of identity is formed   (knowing she/he is at the end of the day);   If Unresolved: experiencing role confusion (not knowing who they are)   The may be stuck at this stage when they are 35; this may be demonstrated   by wearing age inappropriate clothing or not acting their age in   other ways)

Ex.

An individual who is older and is still acting like "Lady Gaga" may be in the Role Confusion stage.

or Someone who is older (40's, 50's and beyond and is still dressing like "Madonna" - Role Confusion stage!)

6. **Intimacy vs. Isolation (19-35 years old);** Intimacy – /Think: intimate relationships; It implies connectedness as far as relationships are concerned (these could include professional, social or sexual relationships); If resolved: develop Intimacy; If not resolved – results in isolation (inability to form stable relationships)

   Memory Hint: Intimacy - Intimate relationships

7. **Generativity vs. Stagnation (30-50 years);** Think next generation for generativity; If Resolved: (This means if the individual is settled in their life personally/professionally, the natural progression is a growing concern for the next generation; Note; You don't need to be a parent in order to feel a caring for the next generation.; If unresolved: Stagnation – A sense of being stuck; being self -indulgent and uncaring

8-**Integrity vs. Despair (50+years – the end of life);** - This is a life review; If resolved: there is a sense of integrity in your life – Accepting your accomplishments/being happy about what you achieved; You can also view it as a sense of Authenticity - there is a sense of meaning and quality in one's life.

If Unresolved – this creates a sense of extreme sadness and regret over your life choices/situations.

In sum, with regard to all these stages, they represent a solid way of interacting with and comprehending your clients. For ex., if you happen to be working with a client that is disconnected from others, you may be able to better understand this individual, as he/she appears to be in the "Intimacy vs. Isolation" stage. Social Withdrawal may serve as a huge indicator of a person's pathology and state of mind.

Similarly, if you're working with an individual that is "drifting through life"; is permanently stuck in the adolescent mode (i.e., dressing in an age-inappropriate manner; indulging in age-inappropriate activities); that person may be stuck in the "Identity vs. Role Confusion" stage. Knowing Erikson will help you know that and work with that client better.

If you provide services to an elderly individual and that person is rooted in their past misfortune; that will help you demonstrate further sensitivity to him/. her, as he/she may be going through the "Despair" portion of the Ego Integrity vs. Despair stage.

After Erikson, one of the most important theorists is Piaget, who developed the Theory of Cognitive Development. His theory arose out of his own personal observations of children and from that he developed schemas of their thought pattern.

Cognitive Theory of Development: - Piaget

After Erikson, one of the most important theorists is Piaget, who developed the theory of Cognitive Development. His theory arose out of his own observations of children and what he developed of their thought patterns - schemas.

Memory Trick: Piaget:

Think: Operational:/ (Mental Operations) / O.P.P. Song - :)

How this translates itself over on the exam: If a theory scenario has to do with learning how to think; concept development, chances are it is Piaget.

Piaget constructed his theory based on the observations he conducted of children.

He felt that learning is a result of mental connections that are formulated by children.

His theory focuses on the formation of concepts in the child's/teenager's learning process.

Sensory-Motor Stage: (0-2); Memory Trick: The age before 2; the Terrible Two's.

In this stage, the infant explores the world, based on his senses; namely taste (sucking), touch, smell, etc. A crucial component of this stage is the development of "Object permanence", which is a notion that objects continue to exist despite their absence. For example, the infant's mom may hide a toy out of reach and the infant perceives that it is gone forever. When object permanence/object constancy is developed, a child recognizes that even though a toy may have been placed in a different room, it continues to exist.

"Playing Peek - A - Boo" - If mommy hides her face, does she still exist? If the child thinks that she doesn't, they haven't developed a sense of Object Permanence.

Pre-operational Stage: (2-7): Memory Trick: (2 yrs. - Terrible Two's).
One of the crucial parts of the stage is the age group with which it is associated: 2 may be thought of as the "terrible two's and therefore in this particular period, the focus is entirely upon the self (Egocentrism)

Children do not yet have concrete schemas (Mental representations) to identify objects, however that ability is being formulated.

For example, children don't have the sense of Conservation, which means that if they see the same amount of liquid poured into two different sized glasses, they will think that there is more liquid in one glass because it is larger.

There is a concept of **Animism** * (think inanimate objects) that is associated with this stage. Animism - means attributing human-like characteristics to inanimate objects. For ex. The child may think that if a stuffed animal fell, the stuffed animal got hurt.

Magical Thinking: Magical Thinking is a concept that means that by thinking about something, they may cause it to happen. For example, if the child has bad thoughts about "mommy" and Mommy gets sick, they think that they caused the illness.

Concrete-Operational Stage: (7-11/like the popular food chain :))

In this stage, object permanence is fully developed; the child has also acquired a sense of centration, conservation; seriation (number order) and whole/part relationships. The child can identify objects using proper names and has a concrete sense of what they objects represent. They start to understand Irreversibility. which means that they acknowledge and comprehend the meaning of the finality of death/an irreversible state.

Formal Operations: (11-18); In this stage, children/tweens/teens are more capable of responding for abstract thought processes, i.e., deductive reasoning, hypothetical situations. Their thinking is not concrete, and they can construct hypothetical scenarios in their imagination

Freud's Psychosexual Stages of Development

Freud is the father of Psychology and many of his constructs will be prevalent in the applications of social work. The emphasis of his theory of development is based on psychosexual stages and their influence in the stages of an individual's progress.

Since the sexuality is centered around pleasure and gratification, we will consider each stage as framed by the pleasure principle.

Janet Jackson: "The Pleasure Principle" Song!

This will be applicable in our theory of Freud, as in each stage, the individual will derive pleasure from the stage he is involved in.

Oral Stage - 0 - 1 years old: The primary source of pleasure/gratification is focused on the mouth. Memory Trick: Oral - Mouth; The infant derives a beneficial sensation from their association with the mouth (i.e., holding items in the mouth, sucking, etc.) The unsuccessful resolution of this stage occurs in what's known as a fixation: / An oral fixation - is a preoccupation with the mouth as the primary source of pleasure; The individual with an oral fixation smokes/eats/chews fingernail incessantly.

Anal Stage - 1 -3 years old: The benchmark of 3 is important, as it is associated with toilet training and the retention/release of the bowel. Thus, the primary source of stimulation/satisfaction occurs from a mastery and control of the bowels; release and control; The unsuccessful resolution: results in the "Anal retentive personality". People that are anal retentive have to sustain a sense of order or control (Control is the driving force here!) by having everything done in a specific manner; excessive cleanliness, orderliness, compartmentalizing.

Phallic Stage - 3-6; Memory Tip: (Phallic - P- for Private Parts:) The phallic stages is defined by the channelling of the sexually inappropriate desires into more socially acceptable channels. Children at this stage are staring to be cognizant of their genitals. In that, they start exploring their genital area via self-stimulation. At this stage, they are also very vulnerable to sexual exploitation because they do not understand their genitals parts completely or what the genital parts can do. Exploitation - meaning sexual abuse or incest, etc.

Latency stage - 6-12; Memory Tip: The sexuality is dormant/latent; meaning asleep; this mean the individual is taking a break from sexuality and moving on to socialization.

Blending sexual desires into more socially appropriate channels; more social connections. In this stage, the child is likely to move away from the sexual component and focus on the building of social relationships. (Ex. Boys or girls are yucky at this stage: LOL!)

Genital Stage: (12+ years); Libido/Sexual interest is once again centered on the genitals and successful integration occurs when sexual desire is blended with affection.

(Ex. First serious intimate relationship.)

Freud also developed the Structural basis of the psyche, which consists of 3 parts:

Structural basis of the psyche: Freud believed that our mental activities is constructed by **3 functions.**

Function 1: Id - the pleasure principle; think of the Id as I - for

"I want".

Ego - is the reality principle of the mental thought process. It refers to "practical measure, such as "the reality of what one can have or not have".

Superego: - is the negotiator or mediator between the Id and the Ego.

Refer to the cartoon on the following pages

"Think of the Id - as the angel in the cartoon; I want; please give me etc./ Remember "Id" a standing for "I"/ " I want"... :)

"Think of the Ego - as the part of the mind that says the opposite to what the Id wants: "You can't have".... "It's not right", "It's not appropriate".

Superego - is the Negotiator: It is a kind of "referee" between the Id and the Ego!

William Shatner - :) Priceline/ "The Negotiator" :) - Superego...

The Superego is like the conscience. It channels the conflict between the Id and the Ego into more socially acceptable behaviors.

- Freud also developed **Defense Mechanisms** and his daughter, Anna Freud continued the work.

Defense Mechanisms: Defense mechanisms are unconscious, uncomfortable, anxiety-producing drives which may feel uncomfortable or displeasing to the individual. Therefore, they drive them away by developing Defense Mechanisms. The individual may feel guilt, shame at having these thoughts or feelings and therefore may cover them up by using defense mechanisms. They may also be thought of as protective mechanisms.

gg106670047 GoGraph ©

Ex. Rationalization:

1. **Rationalization:** - Making excuses: Example. I bought something that was meant for somebody else, and I want to keep it: "Rationalization - I tell myself that she doesn't know that I bought it anyway.

2. **Denial** - Refusing to believe a situation/event. (Ex. Denying that a relationship is over.)

3. **Projection** - Placing your own feelings unto somebody else: / Ex. Saying that someone is jealous when you, yourself are jealous.

4. **Reaction Formation:** - Turning an emotion into its direct opposite: Example: When you really hate someone, you go overboard and act very nice to them.

5. **Sublimation:** - Channelling an unacceptable emotion into a socially acceptable outlet: For example: You're angry at your boss, but you can't go and yell and them, so you channel that anger into taking a boxing class.

6. **Introjection:** Taking someone else's emotions into yourself. (Ex. Absorbing someone's pain/disease as your own.)/ Memory trick: Intro - taking into yourself.

7. **Undoing: -** replacing an unacceptable thought or behavior and going overboard in compensating for it. (For example; taking back an uncomfortable action/behavior. - Ratting out a co-worker and then going up to the boss and saying that the co-worker is nice after all.)

Undo - Undoing/taking back what you did!

8. **Intellectualization:** - when an individual avoids uncomfortable emotions by looking at them more logically. Ex. When someone passes away, he/she says: "Well, they were old, anyway".

9. **Isolation of Affect:** - Removing the emotion (affect) from an unacceptable impulse, idea. (For example, if a loved one dies; not crying, not grieving or reacting at all.)

10. **Projective Identification:** - a form of projection used by persons with borderline personality disorder: unconsciously taking in others' behavior as a reflection of one's own.

"Feeling responsible for someone's behaviors and therefore taking it as one's own behavior. For ex. Your co-worker messed up at work, but you take it as you failed at work.

11. **Displacement: Memory trick**: To displace; to place blame; to take things out on someone less threatening. For example: You're angry at your boss and you go home and yell at your spouse

12. **Repression: Mental blocks**; Suppressing painful information by forgetting it.

13. **Splitting:** Perceiving a person as all good or all bad. Not being able to synthesize all the parts of the individual; the good, the bad, the ugly :) (Common in Borderline Personality Disorder.)

Kohlberg's Theory of Moral Development:

Kohlberg postulated his theory of development, as being defined by morality/ a sense of right and wrong.

In that, he developed this 3-stage theory that is important to know:

Memory Trick: (Convention - stands for social expectations/sense of right and wrong!) /Another Memory Trick: K- Kohlberg: (K- Sound/ K sounding - Conventional:

Pre-Conventional Stage: (Think pre- before/prior - refers to the 1st stage of development.

In this stage, morality is defined by the action that avoids punishment. For example, if a child's behavior results in consequences from the parents, he/she learns to avoid this behavior. Moreover, he/she believes that the right action will be the one that avoids punishment in the future. Ex. A child hits another child, and his parents punish him. Now, the child thinks that the right behavior ("Not hitting") is the one that will avoid being punished, as opposed to the right behavior being "Not hitting".

Conventional Stage: (middle stage).

In this stage, children/teens believe that morality is defined by the actions of peers. Therefore, if a friend/boyfriend/girlfriend uses a behavior that is deemed acceptable by the individual, he/she adopts that behavior as the morally ethical one. (Ex. If my friends think it's appropriate to do drugs, which must be the right thing to do.)

Post-Conventional Stage: (Post - means after; last stage.)

In this stage, individuals learn the truly ethical code of behaviors. They learn to recognize that models of appropriate behavior/ the moral code are channelled by what is deemed as socially acceptable in society. (Ex. if everyone follows the speed limit as stated by law, that's the right thing to do.)

Margaret Mahler Object Relations Theory:

- The best way to remember this theory is using "Mahler - standing for "Mom".

The role of the mother is also going to be crucial in this stage.

The entire theory is shaped by the infant separating/individuating from the mother

Object relations - meaning how the object: /child forms his/her relationships based on these early interactions with Mom/caregiver.

1. **Autistic stage** - Birth to 1 mo.: Remember the term Autistic as the Autistic Disorder:

- At this stage: The infant does not recognize the mom as a separate being. She/he is in their own world (sometimes like an Autistic individual)

2. **Symbiosis: 1 - 5 months**: The child is still fused/symbiotic with the mom. He/she is starting to recognize the mom as a separate object, however. The word Symbiotic - means closely connected; Here the child is still closely connected/fused with the mom but is starting to recognize the mom as separate.

Separation-Individuation:

3. **Differentiation 6-9 months:** The child differentiates/shows independence by crawling, but Mom is still in the vicinity. (Same room).

4. **Practicing 9-14 months:** The child separates by walking, which is one of the developmental milestones at that age. Mom is still in the room making sure he/she is all right and the child does not go too far, to make sure that he/she does not drift too far away from Mom!

5. **Rapproachment 14-24 months** the child starts to walk away but looks back to make sure that Mom is still there. This stage is crucial, as according to Mahler, it may directly connect to "borderline personality disorder". If the phase is handled properly, the child will develop a healthy sense of boundaries/ attachment. If the mother reacts poorly or starts worrying when the child is walking away, the child may develop a poor sense of boundaries/attachment - (Poor boundaries are associated with borderline personality disorder.) Or, if the child continuously looks back to make sure that the mom is still around, he/she could develop poor boundaries.

6. **Object Constancy (about 24 months):** The individual achieves a permanent sense of the mother as a permanent fixture in her life. (Similar to the concept of Object Constancy in Piaget, however the object is the mother.)

Chapter 7

The Other Theories:

Erikson, Piaget, Kohlberg, Freud and Mahler are going to be the most important theorists considered for the exam.

However, there are many theorists that will be considered:

Maslow - Hierarchy of Needs:

Self-Actualization (aspirations to grow/become the "best version of yourself"

Esteem (Self-esteem)

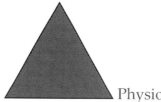

Love   Physiological Needs/Safety

Maslow believes that the health (including physiological needs, such as food and medications) and Safety are paramount to other needs on the Hierarchy.

Following that, the most important need is relationships/Love, which creates a sense of belonging and connection. After that, is a need for Esteem, which is the sense of oneself respect, value.)

The need for Social Connection is real!!

One of the most excruciating punishments is Solitary Confinement because the prisoner is not able to socialize with anybody! This form of punishment is so bad that people can become psychotic, suicidal, aggressive. The Prison system is thinking of doing away with Solitary Confinement as it is that harsh!

So, therefore, according to Maslow and many other theorists/philosophers, Social Connection is crucial to the well-being of others!

Self-Actualization is the last need on the Hierarchy. It means the individuals' capability/desire to grow and develop intellectually, spiritually, etc.

This theory is important in Social Work, as if there is Safety involved on a question on the exam, you will want to address that first. It is the same with Health. Before, you make any type of assessment, you need to rule out health/medical conditions.

Carl Jung:

Jung postulated his theory on the "Here and Now".

Jung postulated his theory on the "Here and Now". He, like Freud also believe in the unconscious. He postulates that there are different archetypes in the person's unconscious.

1- The Sage; - Free thinker; their intellect is the reason for their existence.

2- The Innocent: - They are involved in self-improvement; they are also invested in seeing the positive in everything and everyone.

3- The Explorer: - They area wanderer; they love discovering new places and things about themselves.

4- The Ruler: - The leader; a take-charge person.

5- The Creator: - the creator seeks out new things; rebels; independent nature

6- The Caregiver: - The caregiver feels stronger than others and is therefore trying to protect others around him.

7- The Magician: - They are constantly developing and changing.

8 - The Hero: - The hero is motivated by power. They are obsessed with winning.

Charlie Sheen - "Winning" :) That's my little joke.

9 - The Rebel: The rebel doesn't consider other people's opinions.

10- The Lover: They are all heart and are all about love.

11- The Jester: Enjoys laughing at himself.

12- The Orphan: The orphan often plays the victim. They constantly feel hurt.

(You don't need to know all the archetypes for the exam, but just be familiar that they exist.)

He also believed in the concept of the Collective Unconsciousness. He felt that every individual has some trait that is reminiscent of our ancestors from the time that people appeared on Earth.

He believed in the concept of the Collective Unconsciousness. He felt that every individual has some trait that is reminiscent of our ancestors from the time that people appeared on Earth.

"We carry in us traits that are reminiscent of our ancestors; "Cavemen and beyond", according to Jung.

Jung - believed in the "Shadow" archetype. This refers to the unconscious aspect of one's personality. It is usually thought of as a negative part of one's characteristics, although it contains some positive parts as well Think - shadow /dark (judgment, aggressive impulses, immoral inklings, fears, irrational desires.)

"The Shadow" Part of us, according to Jung.

Carl Rogers: - Person Centered Therapy:

Person-centered therapy is framed by the belief that every person has a self-actualizing tendency: "Self-actualizing tendency" - means that the person is capable of "more"/of growth and development/of self-improvement.

The way that the "Self-actualizing tendency" develops is through a technique called the "Unconditional positive regard". Unconditional positive regard: - is a technique in which the social worker/therapist shows empathy/understanding through complete acceptable of the patient. They use phrases to praise/support/validate the individual, so he/she feels accepted.

Cognitive-Behavioral Theory: - Beck

This theory focuses on the impact of cognitive representations and cognitive distortions on emotions and behavior.

A common technique of cognitive behavioral therapies is Rational Restructuring:

Rational Restructuring: is eliminating irrational/possibly destructive thoughts and restructuring them into more reality-based thinking.

Reality Therapy: (Glasser): - suggests that human behavior originates from the individual, rather than from outside sources. One of the techniques is on the development of a success identity.

Solution-Focused Therapy: (Bateson, Erickson, Jackson, etc.) - Solution focused therapy is just like it sounds. It's aimed at developing solutions, rather than focus on the individual's problem or issue. In this method, the focus is on the presenting problem. The SW works with clients on specific goal; the Emphasis on small, feasible actions that clients can undertake now. For example, if the client's problem is obtaining a job, the SW may introduce motivation: "On a scale of 1-10, how motivated are you to find a job?" They also suggest other coping mechanisms, such as asking the client what kinds of things they worked on in the past to solve a similar problem.

("The Miracle Question":) is the most famous technique associated with Solution-Focused Therapy: It asks, "What would you think would take place if all your problems disappeared tomorrow?" (For ex., if you won the lotto?)

Bowenian Family Therapy: - Bowen believed that person can only be understood in the relational context. He focused on patterns in family relationships. He further delved into strong connections between family members. According to his theory, a strong ego functioning makes it easier for a family member to separate from the fabric of his family. He believed in healthy boundaries between family members and the need to individuate.

(This is very reminiscent of Mahler's approach in individuals forming healthy boundaries in her Object Relations Theory.)

Role Theory: - is oriented to how the behaviors of individuals are influenced by the roles/status that they hold.

Play Therapy: - Axline: The goal of play therapy is to explore the mind of the child through play. Some of the techniques that may be used are Artwork, games, feeling cards, etc.

Gestalt Therapy: - Perls - the belief behind Gestalt Therapy is that each individual is capable personal responsibility for their own thoughts, feelings, actions. An individuals' gestalts (perceptions of parts as wholes) are what form their needs.

The goal of Gestalt Therapy - is for a client to achieve unity with the various aspects parts of him/herself.; Gestalt therapy: uses the "Empty Chair technique" : The Empty Chair Technique may be thought of as a Role Play: In other words, the individual talks to a "mother, father, brother, sister, lover" as if they are sitting in the chair. However, the chair is, of course, empty. Gestalt therapy also enhances Communication techniques, as it instructs clients to use "I" statements when talking about one another. For ex. "I feel hurt when you...."

Dialectical Behavior Therapy: This is a therapy that is commonly used with people with borderline personality disorder (as well as Bipolar D/O in some instances). It focuses on mindfulness, which is a concept that is widely used in Eastern religious philosophies. " Eastern beliefs emphasize the fact that the mind may be thought of as a "monkey mind", in that it jumps around all over the place. The concept of "Mindfulness" helps the individual "stay in the moment". DBT also works with Emotion regulation, in that it teaches the client "not to react" in the moment and to consider consequences of quick reactions.

EMDR: (Eye Movement Desensitization and Re-processing):

This is a technique that is used with people suffering from post-traumatic stress disorder. In this type of therapy, the individual is asked to recreate the traumatic moment/event in his/her mind and is guided to use "tapping" or eye movements in order to ground them to the present.

Social Psychology Research: (Allport): Social Psychology examine how the behavior of individuals may be influenced by the actual or suggested presence of other people.

Social Exchange Theory: predicts the decision to stay or leave a relationship based on the benefits the relationship holds. (Ex. making a list of pros and cons of staying in a relationship/friendship.)

Social Influence:/Bases of Social Power: (French and Raven)

In order for an individual to have influence over another individual, they must possess some kind of power.

In the popular drama, "Empire", Lucious Lyon is the head and leader of Empire (or Cookie :) depending on how you view it). Therefore, he has power over what happens to the company, his artists' direction, etc.

For us older folks, in the popular show Dynasty in the 1980's, Blake Carrington had the power of his oil company, "Denver Carrington"/ as did Alexis at some point. :)

Coercive Power: - the subject that's influencing the individual has control over punishments.

Reward: - the subject that's influencing the individual has control over rewards.

Expert: The subject that's influencing the individual has some kind of advanced ability or knowledge (an expert).

Referent: - the target likes the influencing agent. Hence, the source of power.

Legitimate: - the target believes that the subject that's influencing him has some kind of legitimate authority.

Informational: - the source of the influence/power is due to the fact that the subject that influences has specific information that is needed.

Cognitive Dissonance: (Festinger:) - It is believed that when individuals have two thoughts that are not consistent with each other, they experience dissonance and attempt to resolve it by either changing their mind/behavior, etc.

Identity Development: /Gender Schema Theory: (Bem): This is an important theory; in that it is believed that a gender identity is a combination of social learning and cognitive development.

Chapter 8

Family Therapy

This subject has also become an integral part of the Exam and therefore needs to be examined thoroughly.

In family therapy, the emphasis is on the family. The family is treated as a whole. The overall presiding belief in Family Therapy is the fact that the differentiation of the family is tantamount to the wellness of the family, as a whole. What does that mean? It means that each member of the family needs to achieve a sense of their his/her own identity in the family, in order to be a functioning individual. It is postulated that if any family member is enmeshed (overly attached) with the family, it will not be good for his/her growth as an individual. Having said that, let us go into the various types of family therapy there are.

Communication Interaction Model: (Bateson et. al.)

The crux of this model is that all behavior is communicative in nature. Therefore, the model looks at how members of the family interact with each other.

Extended Family System: (Bowen): The emphasis here is particularly on differentiation. The individual must have their own separate emotions and feelings and not be suffused with the feelings of the entire family.

Triangulation is a process whereby a third member of the family is involved into a situation in order to diffuse the situation.

Family Projection process: the parental conflicts are transmitted onto the child. This may be explained as having to choose sides during a familial dispute.

Multigenerational process: The dysfunction is perceived as the result of multigenerational dysfunctional patterns of behavior.

Emotional cutoff: This is a procedure in which one of the children cuts their ties off from the family.

Structural Family Therapy: (Minuchin): the key word here is structure. This system believed that there is a certain structure in the family between family members. It spoke to Hierarchies and alignments and coalitions as structures in the family. Coalitions

are formed as alliances within a family, for example, a husband-and-wife power up against a child.

Enactment: is an important process in SFT, in that family members are given an assignment to do a role play to demonstrate relational patterns within a family. The focus is that the result of this role play will be a re-formulation/re-framing of the family system.

Emotional fusion: This happens when the family unit blames one/or more family members for separating/having lives of their own.

Strategic Family Therapy: (Haley):

The emphasis is on communication within families. The primary goal of the therapy is to change the family's transactions and its hierarchies, as well as generational boundaries.

The role of the SW in this model is primarily observation of the familial interactions. Additionally, the SW assigns goals and directives in order to help the family alter their communication patterns.

In Paradoxical Intervention: the focus is on having family members focus on their maladaptive communication patterns in order to recognize how they hinder the family system. For example, if a couple has a pattern of fighting, the SW encourages them to fight, in order to identify and change the fighting routines.

Milan Family Therapy:

In Milan Family therapy, one or two Social Workers may meet with the family while the other social workers observe the sessions through a one-way mirror.

The concept of **Circularity** is used, in that the therapists ask circular questions, such as "On a scale of 1 to 10, how serious was the power struggle you were having the night before?"

Chapter 9

Communication Techniques:

(This chapter is particularly helpful for the LCSW Exam!)

We, as Social Workers need to engage and connect with our clients. Therefore, communication techniques are important. Here are some of them that we use:

Reflection: Reflecting back, echoing what the client said; Also, a form of validation: For ex. if a client tells you about all the stresses they have in their life, you may want to say something like: "It certainly sounds like you're stressed out/overwhelmed".

Clarification: It's also like it sounds; it's gaining more clarity; asking more questions into the client's situation: For example: "Tell me more about that situation..."

Confrontation: This is a watered-down version of the actual word: We can confront a client in a soft way, but also only in situations when a client is with us for a long time, and we established trust and rapport with him/her. For example: If a client wants to lose weight but is out eating hamburgers and Ice Cream every day, "You may want to say, " Matthew, you spoke about losing weight, however you are eating in an unhealthy way on a daily basis."

Active Listening: Listening with intent, mirroring the client's statements (reflecting them back to them or putting a name to what they are experiencing); listening without judgment; repeating the phrase also shows the fact that the SW is hearing what the client said; summarizing (making a summary of what the client said), paraphrasing (putting the statement into one's own words);

Partialization: Breaking down a problem/situation into its smaller components; This is particularly useful when an individual has too many issues that they want to tackle all at once.

Exploring Silence: Silence may be uncomfortable, but it is not to be avoided. Silence gives the client time to reflect on what's being said or to formulate what they are trying to say.

As Clinical Social Workers and in other types of Social Work, we rely on these techniques a lot in order to build a relationship.

As social workers, we may also have to work with **Involuntary clients;** by Involuntary clients, I mean, people that are mandated to come in for services. For example, people on parole or parents involved with Child Protective Services.

We, especially need to work with them in a special way to further provide them with assistance/support. First of all, they need to sign a consent form for our services. Yes, even though, they are mandated. Secondly, they may face a certain form of resistance. In other words, they will not want to be there! We need to "Start where they are"! That means, mirroring their resistance. For example: You may want to say: "Mr. Simpson, I know you don't want to be here "(LOL! / I know, it's not so funny.) However, as long as you are here, let me try to help you."

Communication with non-mandated clients takes on a similar process. The Social Worker wants to be genuine, warm and non-judgmental in order to make the client feel safe. You want to demonstrate "Regard" or Acceptance, meaning that you will support them with their challenges and difficulties. You need to make them feel as if you're on their side and you have their best interests at heart.

You will be working with many different clients. Some will be fearful upon talking or may feel uncomfortable and awkward. Others will be more expressive. In either case, you want to create a **"safe space"** for working with your clients.

Chapter 10

Classical Conditioning:

You may be asking yourself why, as social workers we study Classical and Operant Conditioning. The answer is that this is a method of understanding behaviors. The theorists that developed these theories believed that learning is a series of connections, learned associations and conditioning. So, as an example, if you salivate to your favorite dish, it is an association that you made to smelling the tasty dinner that was made.

shutterstock.com · 1409006447

Pavlov:

Classical Conditioning postulates that learning occurs as a result of a pairing between a Conditioned/previously neutral stimulus - Ex. **Salivation** with the Conditioned Stimulus: **Bell**

In Pavlov's experiment: Dogs salivated naturally to the scent of meat powder. When he started ringing the bell and pairing it with the meat powder, the dogs began salivating to the Bell. - Conditioned stimulus - Bell; Conditioned Response: - Salivating.

PLEASE SEE WRITTEN DIAGRAM:

UCS (Unconditioned Stimulus) - Meat - Produces UCR - Unconditioned Response - Salivation

Conditioned Stimulus - Bell = will now produce Conditioned Response Salivation.

or UCS = Meat - Produced UCR = Salivation

UCR = Bell - now produced CR = which is Salivation.

Explanation:

Previously, the Unconditioned Stimulus - Meat Powder naturally/automatically produced the Unconditioned Response - Salivation (therefore no conditioning/associating/pairing was needed.)

Now, the Conditioned Stimulus - Bell will be produce the Conditioned Response - Salivation as it was conditioned to produce a response.

The Classical Conditioning Principle of Salivating to a Bell **is Stimulus Discrimination**, as the dog distinguishes between which stimulus to salivate to (the bell). (discriminates).

Classical Extinction: - the fading out of a stimulus. For ex. Discontinuing presenting the meat powder - The result would be that the dog would stop salivating to the presentation of the scent of meat powder.

Some techniques in Classical Conditioning:

Systematic Desensitization: This is widely used in the treatment of phobia. In this system, the client is asked to go through a hierarchy of fears, so to speak in order to overcome them. For example, if (s)he is afraid of flying, he/she will start out by pretending them to be in the airplane, listening to the Safety instructions; followed by going to the airport, climbing on to the plane, and etc.

Operant Conditioning: B. F. Skinner

The ABC Model:

A = Antecedent events - occur before B - behaviors.

In turn, these are followed by **C**= consequences.

The Law of Effect - Thorndike:

The Law of Effect states that an event that is followed by a pleasurable activity/situation/praise is likely to be repeated.

For example: If I give my child a favorite treat after she does her homework, she will be more likely to do her homework again.

Principles of Operant Conditioning:

Positive: - adding /Positive Reinforcement: (a reinforcer, for ex. You'll get a reward if you pass your ASWB Exam!)

Negative: - taking away an unpleasant stimulus: /Negative Reinforcement: A wife stops criticizing the husband for not making enough money. After the wife stops the criticism, the husband starts seeking more financial opportunities.

Punishment: (behavior is likely to decrease if something is taken away in response to a negative occurrence.)

Positive Punishment: The addition of an event/situation/item decreases a behavior. For example: Your mother takes away your IPad for skipping school. You stop skipping school, as a result!

Negative Punishment: "The taking away" of an event/situation/item following a behavior decreases that behavior. For example: If a father sends a child to his room when he teases his sister, and this causes the child to stop teasing the sister.

Reinforcement Strategies: What is meant by Reinforcement Strategies? If a reinforcement is delivered regularly, it may lose its effectiveness as the agent will begin to expect it at a certain time. It is for this reason that reinforcement strategies were created.

Types of Reinforcement Strategies:

Continuous Reinforcement: The reinforcement is delivered regularly after a particular behavior. (For ex. Working for two weeks - behavior; Receiving a paycheck - reinforcer)

Ex. of Continuous Reinforcement

Intermittent Reinforcement: The reinforcement is delivered at different intervals. For example: "Gambling" can be thought of as a reinforcement strategy. The gambler does not know when he/she will hit the jackpot; the payout occurs at unpredictable times. Therefore, the gambler may be more addicted to the process, as he/she does not know when the reinforcement will be delivered.

Ex. of Intermittent Reinforcement: - You don't know when you will get the money (Reinforcement).

Chapter 11

Stages of Grief:

Elizabeth Kubler-Ross: -Elizabeth Kubler-Ross developed the stages that an individual may go through as a result of grief/loss.

Grief and Loss are not linear. People may fluctuate in and out of these stages and there is no timetable for getting over the grief-provoking situation.

Denial - A refusal to believe that the situation happened.

Anger - Feeling angry at the situation, or angry at the person that "left" you.

Bargaining - "Bargaining with God" or an unknown figure to bring the person back. This is of course not real bargaining. However, during this stage, you make deals with God that if they bring the person back, you will give up....... X

Depression: - At the depression stage, you've pretty much "gave up hope" and went through the 3 previous stages. At this point, you understand that the person is not coming back, and you become depressed.

Acceptance: - Acceptance is coming to terms with the situation. You may still feel depressed, lost, angry, but you've accepted the situation.

Some of my favorite Artists are Prince Rogers Nelson and George Michael! When they both passed in 2016, I was in the grieving process. The first involved being in Denial that they were gone! I still find it unbelievable, so my grief is non-linear!

Bowlby: Attachment Theory: Memory Trick: Use Bowlby for bond (bonding).

Attachment theory is the belief that there is a lasting, psychological connectedness between human beings. This attachment bond starts when a caregiver provides security for the child.

Different Parenting Styles:

Authoritarian Parenting - think Authority; children are expected to follow rules. If they don't, the consequence is most likely punishment.

Authoritative Parenting: - This style parenting is still based on rules, but the parents are more open to discussion once rules are set up. Once the rules are arranged, the parents are forgiving if expectations are not met.

Permissive Parenting: - Parents have a more free-flowing style. They don't expect as much for their children.

Uninvolved Parenting: - Just like it sounds, the parents are largely uninvolved in their children's lives. There are less rules and almost no discipline This is not a desired style of parenting for the kids. The children thrive on more structure, realistic expectations and demands placed on them.

Chapter 12

Working with Different Demographic Groups and Cultural Diversity:

Why do we need to demonstrate cultural sensitivity with our clients? Not only is it considered good practice and a Part of the Code of Ethics, but it is also important to provide better services for our clients. For example, if we do not understand our clients' culture, we may not be as keenly aware of their differences and therefore may be confused as to how to treat them. The most important way to resolve this issue is to ask the client and/or to familiarize themselves with their culture.

Cultural Characteristics are not to be confused with stereotypes:

A stereotype - is when you base an entire race/culture on one person of that particular culture/racial group /activities etc.

Cultural characteristics are tendencies for a culture/race to act in certain ways due to their traditions/rituals, ways of thinking or acting.

Asians/Pacific:

- less emotionally expressive

- The elder male /grandfather is the ultimate authority figure

- Usually turn to family for support

- Believe in alternative treatment methods: Ex. Acupuncture, Herbs, etc.

Hispanic-Americans:

- excessive emotionality

- shame/stigma associated with obtaining social services/therapy

- belief in religious sacraments/rituals (religious candles) as form of help

- deep sense of family obligation

Black Americans:

- close family unit/ties to one's community; everything is interconnected

- tend to be highly religious

- a strong sense of pride

Arab- Americans:

- Males are considered to be the head of the family.

- Women wear a head dress/hijab and are covered up completely in clothing to display modesty

- Admitting lack of knowledge is shameful.

- It is inappropriate to stand too close to a woman.

Native Americans:

- the tribe is the ultimate authority on all decision-making

- excessive alcoholism

- belief in alternative medicine/faith healers (shamans)

- consider making "eye" contact as rude.

- listeners, as opposed to talkers.

- tend to speak as if telling a story

Ways to work with Persons with Disabilities:

- Provide Reasonable Accommodations (wheelchair ramp, communication devices, assistive hearing devices).

- Do not assume that they can't understand you

- If they come in with a family member/aide, address them first, not their escort.

shutterstock.com · 790582078

Gender/Transgender Population:

- Ask them if they want to be referred to as "He/she". Their gender identity could fluctuate often.

- If they are transgender, do not talk about the original gender unless they want to do so.

- Remember that they go through an extensive period of hormone treatment, counseling, the decision-making process of whether or not to have a sex change and the transition to the overall effects

- If you're uncomfortable with working with them, talk to you supervisor

Ethnocentrism: The belief that one's culture is superior to all others.

Points to Consider:

A- There are many cultural, racial differences, besides the ones that were mentioned. If a person/client acts differently than one would expect of an American individual, attempt to find out about their culture and respect cultural differences.

B - Secondly, Social Workers would want to treat clients accordingly with respect to their culture. For example, it may not be advisable to use first names in initial sessions. In some cultures, which may be considered disrespectful. It is usually better to reserve that type of greeting when a professional becomes more familiar with the client.

C - It is also important to adjust your office space to allow for inclusivity. It should be the type of environment, in which all cultures and racial groups feel welcome. For ex. "gender-neutral bathrooms" are now becoming commonplace to accommodate the "Transgender population".

D - It is a good tactic to be mindful of the power differential that exists between the Social Worker and the client. Clients are astutely aware of this dynamic. It is best to guide your words and actions in a manner that promotes a sense of equality between the two parties. It could be something as simple as the way a Social Worker guides the client into his/her office. If the Social Worker proceeds ahead and does not walk along side of the client, this could cause a huge rift between the client and the Social Worker, as the client will feel disempowered. It is considered to be good practice to set the tone for a degree of sameness on the part of the professional, as well as the client. There will definitely be an imbalance in the relationship, but it is best to minimize as much as possible.

E- It is also important to be aware of different gestures as ways of communicating. One of the biggest misinterpretations that occurs is the use of body language, hand gestures, eye contact, as well as verbal communication as means of expression. Some things "just don't translate well" in the English language. If you're unsure, clarify what the client means.

Important Terms in Cultural Differences and Social Diversity:

Culturagram: - This is an assessment tool that provides a visual representation of the various aspects of an individual and family's culture. For example: Duration of stay in the country, legal status, reason for the immigration, primary language spoken at home, holidays/traditions, educational/work values and etc.

Sociogram: This is a graphic representation of the social links that a person has. It plots the structure of interpersonal relationships within a group situation.

Adolescents: As mentioned before, adolescents through a period of "storm and stress". They may be ruled by their hormones, peer expectations and rebellious inclinations. They also have an air of invincibility, and it is important to take note of that fact. Teenagers feel as if they are capable of anything. They tend to have idealistic/romantic notions and some of these notions will fade as they gain more life experience. They may be interested in trying out new things/ some of which will be harmful. On the flip side, self-esteem may be of primary concern, as the adolescent is "trying on and fitting into their "sense of self/identity. This may include their sense of "psychological self, as well as their sexual identity". During this time, they may relate better to peers, so therefore peer pressure will be central to their experience. It is for those reasons as well that it is particularly important for the SW to establish rapport. The SW should also be aware that "rapport" may take longer with the teenager, as opposed to other demographic groups.

Once the teenage client begins to trust the Social Worker, he/she will come to see him/her as a role model, as well as an authority figure. It is therefore crucial to present a positive image and continue to develop a bond of trust. It is wise to keep "secrets" confidential (for ex. Pregnancy - we are not required to let parents know). And, if we have to report a potentially dangerous situation, (ex .an underage sexual relationship), it is best to be honest with them, so they know what to expect.

When working with adolescents, the social worker must focus on acknowledging feelings. Feelings are changing rapidly at this age, so it's necessary to adjust to the changing emotions. It is particularly crucial to "start where they are". Rapport may take longer than usual, as they may not feel comfortable with disclosing emotional, sensitive information.

If they show a lack of cooperation, it may be wise to engage them in topics that are of interest to them. Some topics that may be: Discussing their favorite music, "YouTube channels', "Apps", and etc. This fosters a sense of trust and familiarity. With adolescents, the Social Worker may be faced with a lot of varying situations (ex. Divorce, sibling rivalry, abuse, sex, self-esteem, substance use, domestic violence, and etc.). The Social Worker will serve as a source of support, a resource for necessary programs and an educator.

The Elderly Client Population: When working with the elderly client population, it is important to take a lot of factors into account.

First of all, you need to be very vigilant to the multiple cognitive, as well as physiological changes that are happening to the clients. These changes may be fluctuating frequently, even on a daily basis. Things to look out for: Memory; Gait; Vision; Hearing.... As a central coordinator of their care, you are responsible for communicating any physical/cognitive changes to the treatment team. (Via case conferences; progress notes.).

It is also important to adjust your working style to fit the client's needs. For ex., "Good lighting is crucial", so paperwork is seen clearly. It is vital to use "Projected speech", so the client can hear you accurately. In other words, speaking slowly is favored over leaning closer to the individuals' ears. The reason for that is that if one leans to the ear, the client may be missing the visual cues associated with speech. It may also be necessary to inquire about the use of hearing aids, visual aids and provide an office with limited distractions.

The aging population tends to have a limited social support network. Therefore, if they value spending the time by reminiscing about their past in lieu of paperwork, the "reminiscing" should take precedence. If is also valuable to engage the clients in routine/structured activities to give them a sense of importance. The aging client may feel the sense of self-esteem rise, as a result of taking care of a plant, animal, etc.

Social workers may also be involved in establishing and/or interpreting Advanced Directives. Special Note: We do not write the Advanced Directives independently. We rely on medical professionals to complete the paperwork; however, we may be involved in establishing or interpreting these documents to our individuals.

Statistically, "white older males" have the highest rate of suicide, so it is noteworthy to pay special attention to their access to means of executing suicide (guns, pills, etc.)

The other factors that are crucial are listed under "Signs of abuse", but generally speaking, it is necessary to closely observe for medication non-compliance, lack of interest in activities or appetite and withdrawal from others.

In sum, this is a fragile, sensitive population and their needs should be treated with care and sensitivity.

Working with Children: -Children are newcomers to the world. Therefore, everything is "exciting and different" to them. Therefore, it is best to nurture their sense of adventure and exploration. This can be achieved by encouraging "safe play"; "verbal praise" and "parallel play - playing alongside others".

As with any other methods, "starting where the client is" is the best tactic. When it comes to children, this may translate itself to the therapist physically getting down on the floor and leading/facilitating the "play therapy". "Play Therapy" was founded by Axline, and it fostered a sense of "expressive play " to uncover a child's sense of rules, communication, sense of the world.

"Play therapy" is a safe way for children to connect with others that is adapted to their own developmental level.

The LGBTQ Population: (Lesbian, Gay, Bisexual Transgender, Questioning).

When working with the LBGTQ population, it is important to note that a systemic lack of inclusivity pervades this community. This starts with the lack of proper terminology listed on documents, to the inequality with entitlement of benefits, as well as a dearth of vocational opportunities. As social workers, these omissions should be our starting points. First of all, we want to begin with the proper terminology:

Gender Identity: is one's gender expression as determined by societal expectations. (For ex. Women are more emotional): A person's gender identity may not necessarily correspond with their original sex.

Sexuality: One's sexual preference/orientation

Non-binary: Feeling neither male, nor female; expression could fluctuate frequently

Cis gender: When one is born into a specific sex and identifies with that sex

Cis-gender privilege: Persons are accepted more freely when they identify with their original, biological sex.

Intersectionality: The understanding that more than one factor can contribute to unjust treatment. (For ex. Being a woman and a lesbian; Being a woman and being Black; Being a Black woman and a lesbian).

Transgender: Transgender is the opposite of cis gender. It means when one is born into a certain sex but does not identify with that sex.

Intersex: The antiquated term is "hermaphrodite". It means that the individual was born with an anatomically atypical sexual abnormality. (For ex. a vagina, as well as a penis).

The ICD-11 (International Classification of Diseases - DSM equivalent) already adopted new terminology for the "Transgender experience". They refer to it as "Sexual incongruence". The DSMV will have to catch up to this reference. "Gender Dysphoria" is still listed in the DSMV and is alluded to as a mental disorder. Social Workers are encouraged to interpret this definition by explaining that the "transgender" is disordered by how society treats them. In order to impart further inclusivity, it is imperative that we advocate for alterations on the current paperwork, such as including the classification of "non-binary" on application/intake forms. We must also promote the use of "gender-neutral" bathrooms to make our clients feel included. Similarly, we must encourage employers and officials to offer the LGBTQ group the opportunities to advance professionally, be eligible for equal housing and other rights that are freely given to others. Our role will mostly be - advocacy; equality; watching for signs of

Suicide/Homicide, mental health, SU, etc. It should be noted that while it is the most difficult experience for the LGBTQ population to "come out", the most harmful experience for them is not being able to express their true selves, either. We must be their champions to encourage self-expression.

Chapter 13

Code of Ethics:

The Code of Ethics is one of the first things you learn as a Social Worker. The Code of Ethics is a general guide of Social Worker characteristics, general accepted practices and ethical procedures.

The Code of Ethics is a legal document and therefore, it may sometimes feel as if it is difficult to understand. It may have terminology/jargon that we are not familiar with. Therefore, I feel there are a lot of misconceptions when interpreting the Code of Ethics. While the Code is not a particularly large document, it is extremely detailed and if you miss an important sentence, you may miss a crucial part of the principle.

The Code of Ethics should be read in its entirety as you need to handle situations, as dictated by the Code of Ethics. The Code of Ethics is a useful tool and a roadmap, as to how to direct your behavior in a professional manner. You should always follow it in your practice, as well as base your answers on it in the exam.

I will present the MOST important standards/situations in the Code of Ethics. When you read it independently, make sure to pay attention to the Standard that is mentioned: (ex. Conflicts of Interests) as well as the way to handle each particular potential ethical situation when working with a client. The different types of standards may be asked on the exam. It is not necessary to memorize all the different standards, but it helps to have a working knowledge of their presence.

A **probable question** you might be asked is to find that answer that describes the "Purpose of the Code of Ethics". The purposes are listed in the beginning. The shortened version of the answer would be that the Purpose consists of standards that Social Workers must hold we to, in order to provide the most ethical treatment for the clients.

Overall, as you approach the practice questions, you will notice that many of them have to do with the Code of Ethics or are somehow inadvertently tied to the Code of Ethics. It is therefore important to be very knowledgeable of them.

Overall Understanding of the Code of Ethics:

In sum, the Code of Ethics states that: the purpose of a Social Worker is to promote the human well-being of others, with a particular focus on the poverty-stricken, vulnerable or underserved populations.

A social worker should be interested in social policy and ways to enhance the laws that govern social work issues/ and clients. In addition, the Social Worker should be concerned with policies that challenge the implementation of equal rights to others.

A S.W. must respect self-determination, promote social justice, emphasize the importance of human relationships, exude integrity and project/provide competence.

A social worker should also respect cultural differences. If a client requires a translator, a professional translator should be provided. It is not acceptable to rely on a family member or an agency staff to translate, as the translation may be inaccurate or biased.

Category: Conflicts of Interests:

A social worker should never barter or enter into Dual Relationships: (This includes both professional and sexual dual relationships.) Dual professional relationships occur when a social worker accepts a clients' services (example doing their taxes) while having a social work/therapeutic relationship. Bartering - means exchanging one service for another. There is a small exception to this matter. In rural areas where bartering is the norm, this arrangement may be acceptable. However, it must be done with the Informed Consent of the client. The social worker must also take responsibility for the securing and implementing the arrangement.

A social worker should never enter into any kind of other relationship with a client/ sexual, romantic, friendship, business, etc. which has the potential to hurt the client. It doesn't matter the relationship stopped the relationship 5, 10, 20 years or any other amount of time after the professional relationship ended. A client should never engage in a sexual relationship with a current client. In situations with past clients, a good rule of thumb is not to pursue this relationship, as it will almost always have the potential to hurt the client.

Similarly, a Social Worker should not leave a job in order to pursue an intimate relationship with one of her clients.

Impairment of Colleagues:

If a social worker suspects a colleague of harmful, self-destructive or destructive behavior (ex. drinking), they should speak to the colleague first. If the colleague does not respond and you continue to suspect that they are engaging in a potentially harmful behavior to clients, you must speak to a supervisor.

Access to Records:

A client has the right to see their own record. However, the Code states that we must give them reasonable access, meaning, enough to satisfy them. The reason that we are discouraged from sharing the entire record is because it may be damaging to the client. You must also offer to interpret the contents of the record, in order to avoid any potential harm/misunderstanding on the client's part. If you feel that the information is extremely damaging, you may refuse the request, but you will have to document that the request has occurred and your rationale for withholding the information.

Privacy: (including Legal Proceedings):

We must never display identifying information about a client in an area where it is viewable by others.

Similarly, we must also not discuss clients in an open, public area, where others may overhear their private information.

(Legal Proceedings) :/ This is referred to in the Privacy Category.

In the case that a legal representative/attorney requests a clients' record, we will apprise them of our respect to confidentiality with the client. However, if it is court ordered that you submit the notes, you can try to withdraw the request if you think it will be damaging to the client. If you are not able to do so, you may ask the court if you can provide a portion of the records and also request that the notes are protected from public view and are kept under seal. If all your efforts are refuted, you must present the documents immediately. You will also need to notify the client that the records were released

(Note: Although this is not reflected in the Code of Ethics, if a supervisor is asked to appear before court, he/she need to seek legal counsel.)

Billing:

We must bill clients amounts that are reasonable for the type of service that we provide. However, if the client is not able to pay, we need to offer sliding-scale amounts, so the clients is able to pay.

In the case that they are unable to pay, even the "sliding-scale fee" and may be a danger to themselves or others, we must continue to treat them free of charge. That arrangement must follow suit, until we can find more affordable resources for them to receive services (Free clinics, etc.). If a client is not in danger and continues not to pay us for services, we can terminate the professional relationship.

The above are the most important categories in the Code of Ethics.

Please read this tool in its entirety so as to familiarize itself with all the categories that it lists. The Code of Ethics was designed to guide and further legitimize our profession.

Special Section about Subpoenas: Subpoenas are requests for a SW to testify or present mental health info/documentation related to the client. They may be used in order to aid the client (ex. the client is suing for emotional damages) or if the client gets into some types of legal situation. If the subpoena arrives from an attorney, it needs to be answered (in writing). However, you are not required to present the information requested. You also cannot reveal that you are servicing this client at your agency, unless more information is requested.

After receiving the subpoena, the SW must notify their client re: the request and then also report the information to the supervisor (if they have a supervisor). Afterwards, they should review the Subpoena (Official written record) and inquire as to who is requesting the information, the authority they have to request the information and the deadline for delivering the info. **If the subpoena is followed by a court order, then the SW must adhere to the rules as directed by the Code of Ethics above in the Legal Proceedings section.**

Jaffe vs. Redmond Case (1996): A police officer shooting a citizen during a domestic violence dispute. The officer is distraught and is sent to the Employment Assistance Program. The family of the deceased sues for wrongful death. The EAP records are requested by the attorney/court, etc., but the SW refuses the present the info. due to confidentiality concerns. The case goes to the Supreme Court and as a result of the SW's actions, the Supreme Court recognizes the "psychotherapy/client privilege".

Chapter 14

Group Therapy:

The most important point to remember in Group Therapy is that the group is treated as a whole. Members come together for a unified issue/purpose. (For ex. Grief/bereavement). Thereby, the group leader/co-leader will have a limited role within the group.

For example: If a member of the group calls the leader/co-leader during the week with a concern, the tactic will be to: "Throw it back to the group"/discuss it within the confines of the group.

How the Answer choice might look on the Exam: "A group member contacts the group leader during the week to discuss concerns with a fellow group member. What should the Group Leader do?

Answer: Redirect/Allow/Encourage the member to bring it up during the group session.

Group Theory:

The most prominent group therapist is Irwin Yalom.

- **Yalom** once again believed that the essence of group therapy is that the group leads itself.

The Defining Principles of Group Therapy:

- The group leader is there as a facilitator.

- The ideal group size is 8-10 members. (For close-ended groups.)

- Open-ended groups are when someone is allowed to attend a group at any time. For ex. - AA- Alcoholics Anonymous can be an open-ended group. It also has the option of being a close-ended group.

- Closed-ended groups are: The group length and sessions are outlined from the beginning.

- Group members are not allowed to come in at later session. The reason is that it may cause a disruption to the group. It is an expected process for group members to confide in one another about potentially sensitive subject. Therefore, if someone is allowed to join at a later date, the dynamic will be changed.

- The only time the group leader becomes very involved is if a group member is expressing a crisis situation (ex. potential for suicidal behavior) or another potentially dangerous situation. In the case of a suicidal disclosure, the group leader will wait until the group is over and then approach the individual. A suicide risk assessment will be performed, as in Individual Treatment.

Think of close-ended groups as the "Closed sign". They are open only to members that start the group from the beginning and finish until the end.

AA - is mostly an open-ended group, with an option for providing close-ended group services.

The members of the groups are also **heterogenous vs. homogenous.**

The **heterogenous members** are people that vary, in terms of age, intelligence level, etc.

Homogenous members are those members that are more alike, in nature (age, intelligence level.)

Groups consisting of homogenous members are more likely to be successful.

The reason for this phenomenon is because it is helpful (especially in the beginning) if people are the same age, have same cultural references, the notion is they will relate better to one another.) The group members will still have different opinions; however, it is important to gather people of a specific age group, intelligence level, etc.

Group Resistance: Group resistance occurs when a group member stop participating, either due to the feeling that his/her problem is less difficult than other members' or that another group member is dominating the group. Jealousy may also occur that the group leader is spending more time with a different individual. Therefore, the other member will close up/show resistance and stop or decrease participating in the discussions.

The Boston Model of Group Development:

Preaffiliation: The group members are getting to know one another and are unsure about being part of the group. All the conversations are being directed at the group leader. The group leader or other members are at risk of being tested.

Power and Control: The group gets acclimated with one another. The group gains a hierarchy, in that roles and ranks are determined. There may be hostility, jealousy, withdrawal from the group. This stage is just like it sounds Power and Control.

Intimacy: Group formation/unity; A commitment is made to the group.

Differentiation: Cohesion; group members serve to support one another; there is more room for "opening up"; less hierarchy conflicts. Different personality types start to emerge.

Separation: A feeling of abandonment may result. Conflicts may resurface. In this stage, the Group Leader becomes more central to the group. He or she prepare the group for termination, as well as plans outside of the group.

The Tuckman Model of Group Formation:

1- **Forming:** - the group members are getting to know one another; most of the comments/questions are being directed to the Group Leader. At this stage, the team members will start to learn how to work as a team.

2- **Storming -** At this stage, the group will begin to test boundaries. This may manifest itself by the members questioning the purpose of the group. Also, like the "Power and Control" stage in the Boston Model, dominant and passive personalities will start to emerge. That means, that some members, as more naturally outgoing will take over the conversations, while others will fade into the background.

3- **Norming:** At this point, the team will start to get to know one another. They may develop relationships outside of the group. This will be followed by progress in the group.

4- **Performing: -** At this point, the group would have reached their end goal. The team should perform (carry out tasks/activities they are given), without conflict.

5- **Adjourning:** - The group will start to disband during this stage. Many of the group members will find this challenging as any unknown situation is difficult. Therefore, conflicts may re-arise, as the members may not be able to cope with the changes that are happening. At this point, the group leader would have to get involved again.

Group Think: Groupthink is a phenomenon that occurs when the group members start to think alike. The point of the group is to share, discuss, offer different opinions.

Groupthink is not a positive occurrence.

Johari Window:

The purpose of the Johari Window experiment/technique is to make the Quadrants (or in this case Circles) "Blind, Unknown and Hidden" "Open to Others". It is useful in a group structure as individuals open themselves up to other members in an effort to heal/grow.

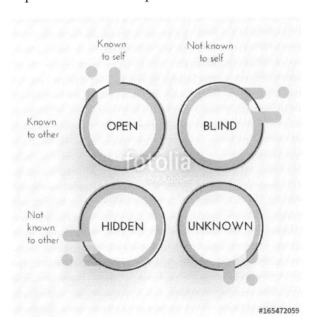

#165472059

The key to Group Therapy: is to throw everything back to the group. The Group Leader should encourage all issues to be discussed amongst group members. This includes if a group member wants to separate from the group.

Chapter 15

DSM V

The DSM V- is named that way for a reason. Diagnostic: refers to the diagnoses that are listed in the DSMV; Statistics- the set criteria and time frame for the symptoms. <u>The Diagnostic and Statistical Manual of Mental Disorders (5th edition).</u> is a useful guide of diagnoses that help you understand your clients' diagnoses and disorders? It becomes particularly helpful in the Assessment process, as the treatment modality/intervention may be based on the diagnosis.

It is also **useful as you may be asked** to **identify a diagnosis** for your client for billing purposes.

The DSM V lists diagnoses by classifying them into types of disorders.

Concurrently, the DSM V lists specific symptoms and the time frame the symptoms last to make an accurate diagnosis.

It is crucial to use the DSMV to pinpoint the duration and types of symptoms a client may have. Some situations may be developmentally or socially appropriate. Also, as such, for example, if a person is stressed out for a week due to finances or a medical situation, it does not mean h/she has a diagnosis, such as Generalized Anxiety Disorder. It is important to assess the client's symptoms and the time frame accurately, so as not to attribute a diagnosis that may not exist. That could cause stigma and vulnerability in an individual. It is also crucial in order to prevent over-medication.

Duration is key in establishing/identifying a diagnosis. For ex., if in the previous example, if the same client has been stressed out due to finances, medical conditions for a period of over 6 months, he/she is more likely to have **<u>Generalized Anxiety Disorder</u>**. Other symptoms must be present, such as restlessness, general state of unease, body tension/muscle aches, lack of concentration and insomnia.

It's the same thing with Depression. If a person comes in and reports feeling sad, it does not necessarily mean he/she has a diagnosis. For a diagnosis of Major **Depressive Disorder** to be established, a person must display symptoms of depressed mood, changes in appetite and sleep, loss of pleasure in usual activities that used to be enjoyable, lack of concentration, suicidal thoughts. These must last for a period of 2 weeks or more.

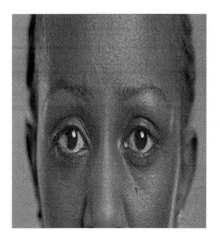 

(Despite being so popular, beautiful and famous, Princess Diana often looked sad :()

The very-handsome model/actor, Ryan Phillipe came out with a public disclosure of his Depression diagnosis. I think it is a very brave thing to do and I commend him for it. I also think it's so important to raise awareness to mental health disorders and by the same token to achieve Mental health parity in Health Insurance matters. For those of you who may not be familiar with the concept of MH parity, it refers to equal treatment by health insurance companies for mental, as well as physical disorders.

The most important disorders that are going to be important for the exam are:

1 - Generalized Anxiety Disorder

2- Depression

3- Schizophrenia and types of Schizophrenia

4- Bipolar I and Bipolar II disorder

5- Intellectual Disabilities (formerly Mental Retardation.)

6 - Personality Disorders

- We already discussed Generalized Anxiety Disorder and Major Depressive Disorder.

The other type of Depression is called **Dysthymia** or **Persistent Depressive Disorder**.

In order to be diagnosed with Dysthymia, a client must manifest depressive symptoms for at least 2 years or longer.

Schizophrenia - is characterized by hallucinations/auditory/visual/perceptual (voices, images, sensations that other people do not see) and delusions - false beliefs, disorganized thinking. Symptoms last for at least a period of 6 months or more. 2/3 symptoms need to be present.

With Schizophrenia, individuals may respond to internal stimuli (voices, visual images or other perceptions that other people don't see), but those sensations will seem real to the individual.

Schizophrenia may also be understood as a general lack of awareness. The affected persons may not have a sense of their own body and deem them as disparate from that of their mind and their cognitive experience. It is most probable that it is for this reason they will neglect their personal hygiene and their physical needs. (A type of "out of body-experience".)

The Schizophrenia Spectrum:

1. Schizophreniform: The individual exhibits the same symptoms as that of schizophrenia, but the length of symptoms is at least for 1 month and is less than 6 months. Schizophreniform may be triggered by high stress. The individual displays the same symptoms as in Schizophrenia (Hallucinations, delusions, disorganized speech), but the condition is less than 6 months.

2. Brief Psychotic Disorder: The episode may last 1 day and less than a month. The symptoms are also delusions, hallucinations, disorganized speech.

Types of Schizophrenia:

1. Catatonic Schizophrenia - The individual demonstrates almost a trance-like state. He/she may sit/stand in one spot; may not be able to move or speak etc.

Delusional Disorders:

Grandiose Delusional Disorder: - the false sense that one's own self is superior to others

Persecutory Delusional Disorder: - the false sense that one is being persecuted against

Paranoid Delusional Disorder - a preoccupation with other's motives; constant suspicion about others; the persistent belief that others should not be trusted.

Jealous Delusional Disorder - the constant false belief that one's mate is being unfaithful.

Bipolar Disorder: - Bipolar I and Bipolar II Disorders were previously referred to as Manic Depression. What is Mania: Mania can be a very dangerous state, in which the individual displays a very expansive sense of self, heightened mood and emotions (highly energetic and exhilarated), as well as a possible reduced need for sleep. In this state, a person may engage in extremely risky type of activities, for example, risky sex, drinking, using drugs, overspending. The individual may also be a potential risk for suicidal attempts. Mania is longer than Hypomania; Mania - lasts an average from 1 week to 3 months.

In **Bipolar I Disorder, 1** or more manic episodes is present, as well as possible depression. The person may shift from mania to depression rapidly. Mania lasts an average of 1-3 months.

Bipolar II: In Bipolar II Disorder, an individual will display 1 hypomanic episode (Hypomania lasts for 4 days) and also a Major Depressive episode (which is 2 wks.)

Cyclothymic Disorders: - think cycles; Major Depressive episodes, with at least 1 hypomanic episode. The Disorder lasts for a period of 2 years.

Personality Disorders: -

A word about Personality Disorders. They are life-long conditions. They are very difficult and almost impossible to treat. An individual with a Personality Disorder will want to be fully invested in the treatment process. People with Personality Disorders can be very difficult clients to serve. The Personality Disorders are now subdivided into 3 Clusters, as per the DSMV.

Cluster A: - includes the disorganized, paranoid, eccentric disorders: (Schizotypal, Schizoid, Paranoid Personality Disorders)

Cluster B: - dramatic, emotional or erratic disorders. (Anti-social personality disorder, Borderline, Histrionic and Narcissistic Personality Disorder.)

Cluster C- Anxious and fearful behavior. (Dependent, Obsessive and Avoidant Personality Disorder.)

Cluster A Disorders: (Disorganized, paranoid, eccentric.)

Schizotypal Personality Disorder: The person demonstrates odd behavior and magical thinking. They push people away because of their odd cognitive beliefs. (Note: You may remember magical thinking from Piaget's pre-operational stage. As a clarification, when it applies to children, the state of magical thinking is absolutely normal, as the child is developing concepts. However, when it pertains to an adult, it is absolutely abnormal and is bizarre.)

Magical thinking refers to the fact that a person may feel as if his thoughts influence reality. For ex. he/she may believe they can cause a hurricane simply by thinking about it. (S)he may also believe that (s)he has the ability to affect a person's actions. It is categorized as irrational thinking and needs to be treated as such.

In the popular 60's show, "Bewitched" and the subsequent movie, "Bewitched", Samantha can twitch her nose and concentrate very hard to make things happen. (Alas, how I wish that was true.) LOL. However, when an individual distinctly believes that he/she can create things just by thinking about them, that is absolutely abnormal and, in this case, constitutes a personality disorder.

Schizoid: A person is a total loner and does not care to form relationships. He/she is mainly void of emotions and is cold in nature.

Paranoid Personality Disorder: (Cluster A) The person is constantly suspicious of others.

There's been a lot of controversy about Michael Jackson, which we don't need to go into. On a personal note, I still love him and have strong opinions on his life and character. (If you'd like to discuss outside this book, please e-mail me :)

On a very different note, he was a very complex person, who was very difficult to assess, especially without knowing him in person.

One of his bizarre behaviors was constantly wearing a face mask outside and sleeping in an Oxygen chamber. Were these signs of a Paranoid Personality Disorder? He definitely appeared to be a germaphobe but appearing in a face mask constantly was excessive. In any case, he exhibited a lot of odd behaviors that are not consistent with "regular" behavior. I will never know if Michael Jackson had a diagnosis. I don't know if wearing a face mask all the time was indicative of a "Paranoid Personality Disorder", but for our purposes, let's use this as an example to remember this particular type of disorder. Long live Michael Jackson's legacy and Rest in Peace our dearest King of Pop!

Cluster B: Disorders: (Dramatic, emotional or erratic disorders.)

Narcissistic Personality Disorder: (Cluster B) The person is basically in love with himself; he/she thinks that the world revolves around them; he may not recognize the emotions of others; grandiose delusions are possible. Persons diagnosed with NPD also experience a hypersensitivity to rejection and criticism. Unconsciously, it's rooted in extremely low self-esteem. However, the individual does not recognize his/her self-esteem issues projects an extremely self-assured facade.

Borderline Personality Disorder: Someone with BPD has poor or no boundaries. (Therefore, the stage of "Rapproachment" in Mahler is applicable here. The child in the Rapproachment stage may constantly look back to make sure the mother is watching. In Mahler's understanding, this constitutes a possibility of poor or enmeshed boundaries. Rapproachment may result in borderline personality disorder, according to Mahler's theory). In addition, someone with BPD may have a sense of "Splitting" (Splitting - is an inability to bring together both positive and negative qualities of the self/others). In other words, the person thinks in "black and white" terms.

For example: He/she may put an individual on a pedestal, but then at a perceived imperfection, s/he may dismiss that person as totally bad!

Thus, individuals with BPD have a "Love/hate" relationship with others. This may translate itself over to a feeling of demand/entitlement. They may criticize the SW all throughout the session and then, at the end, praise them and need them. They also possess a "what I describe" a push/pull personality, in that they crave closeness and intimacy and push it away at the same time.

Anti-social Personality Disorder: - This disorder targets adults. It involves a general disregard of people rules and laws. It results in criminal behavior and there is no remorse experienced by the person that inflicts this behavior.

Histrionic Personality Disorder: Excessively emotional; drama queen. (Cluster A)

My doggie, Princess is quite a drama queen when it comes to having her bowl full all the time! So is Snoopy! Historionic Personality Disorder? Hmmmm... May be who knows? But for our purposes, we will think of them as drama queens!

Cluster C Disorders: (Anxious/fearful behavior.)

Dependent Personality Disorder: The person is unable to function independently; relies on others for all help.

Obsessive-Compulsive Disorder: This designates the need for control. The person may manifest that need by having everything in obsessive order or obsessively clean. They may also manifest compulsions, which are extreme needs to do something: For ex. Lock the door 100 times before he leaves; Wash their hands 100 times before they go out, etc.

Avoidant Personality Disorder: The main difference between this personality disorder and Schizoid Personality Disorder is that in Avoidant Personality Disorder, the individual desires relationships. However, he/she fears being criticized and rejected and therefore pushes them away/avoids them.

Obsessive Personality Disorder This is not to be confused with obsessive compulsive disorder. This happens when a person is perfectionistic and demonstrates rigidity in his/her routines and procedures

Types of Anxiety Disorders:

Panic Disorder: This type of disorder occurs when a person has more than one panic attack. Symptoms may include a feeling of the chest being squeezed, difficulty in breathing, racing thoughts, pounding heartbeat, sweating, an intense feeling of fear. Panic disorder is often confused with a heart attack. If an individual thinks that he/she has these symptoms, he/she need to go to the doctor or an ER to make sure to get the accurate diagnosis. - (A common treatment technique for a panic attack is to instruct the client to start breathing and write what is happening to him/her.)

Agoraphobia: Intense fear of being outside the house.

Separation Anxiety: Persistent and excessive stress when away from home or far away from attachment figures.

Selective Mutism: Failure to speak in specific social situations

Social Anxiety Disorder: An extreme fear of being around others; excessively shy; and fear of being judged.

Separation Anxiety: An excessive fear when separated to the person/situation they person is attached to.

Obsessive-Compulsive Disorders: Obsessive-Compulsive Disorders: Intrusive thoughts and compulsive behaviors (ex. need to wash hands repeatedly); a need for control.

Hoarding Disorder: Having a hard time getting rid of possessions; hanging on to things and a fear of letting go of them.

Thrichotillmania: Excessive need of hair loss/pulling out the hear.

Impulse Control Disorders:

- Impaired impulses.

-Becoming angry and explosive easily.

Oppositional Defiant: becoming irritable very easily; irritable mood; Defiant - just like it sounds; symptoms last for more than 6 months; usually begin before a child is 8. Conduct Disorder: -more associated with children; problems with societal rules (problems with law, etc.).

Anti-Social Disorder: - more associated with adults; 18 and above; extreme problem with rules, laws; no remorse

Intellectual Disabilities: Intellectual Disabilities are defined by a less than average I.Q. (less than 100) and limited functioning skills (ex. personal hygiene, academic, domestic, travel, etc.)

There are 4 types of Intellectual Disability:

Although the **DSMV** did away with the I.Q. designations; these are their approximate I.Q. levels and Mental Ages, as a frame of reference.

Mild: - approximate I.Q. of 75-100; M.A. - Mental Age approximately 5-7 or more

Moderate: - approximate I.Q. of 35 - 55 -   Mental Age   approximately 3-4

Severe -   approximate I.Q. of 20-40   - Mental Age   approximately 2-3

Profound - approximate I.Q. - below 20   -   Mental Age   approximately 1 yrs old or less

The reason that I.Q. levels are estimations are because it is an extremely lengthy process to administer Intelligence Testing to measure I.Q. For example, the Wechsler Intelligence Scale (WAIS-R) is a 4-hour exam that the individual needs to take in order to get an IQ level. It would be exceptionally difficult for an individual with cognitive disabilities to sit through this type of exam. The definition of cognitive abilities are functions having to do with information-processing, memory recall and attention span. Depending on the individual tested, he/she may be able to focus on this testing measure for an average of 2 hours, at best.

Special Note: Until the 1980's, individuals with Intellectual/developmental disabilities were grossly misplaced in institutionalized settings. These settings were inappropriate for them because they did not account for the diagnoses/disorders when admitting these clients. The former talk show host, Geraldo Rivera, exposed the living conditions in one of the institutions, Willowbrook. Willowbrook was located in Long Island, N.Y. What he found was that the clients were severely abused, denied of foods, found sitting in their own urine/feces; robbed of their right to privacy and other individual rights.

Because of this exposure, clients with Intellectual Disabilities, Autistic Spectrum Disorder, Down's Syndrome were removed from the institutions and placed into smaller group homes. (ICF's - Intermediate Care Facilities), which housed an average of 20 people for a residential unit. Later on, during the 2000's the clients were placed into even smaller facilities, IRA's - Individualized Residential Alternatives that averaged 7 people per home.   The clients were also afforded the opportunity to attend vocational/educational programs (Day Habilitation Programs) in order to assist them with their functional skills and offer consistency and continuity of care with their individualized goals.

These types of settings (IRAs, as well as the Day Hab's) placed a premium on the clients' care by providing more individual attention, specific programs, the enforcement of individual rights and the shift to a better quality of life.

This is one of the reasons that it's important to place individuals in the least restrictive setting for them. "Least restrictive" means that it promotes independence and bases itself on their level of functioning/individualized abilities. The notion of the "least restrictive setting" may be mentioned on the exam. Therefore, it is important to understand its concept.

- Persons with Intellectual Disabilities are not completely disabled. Some can speak, work, play, engage in social relationships. Others are more limited, in terms of functioning, particularly adaptive/ADL (Adult Living Skills). Their abilities are dependent on their functioning level. They can learn skills with prompting.

PICA -

PICA is a disorder that commonly occurs with people with Intellectual Disabilities. PICA is a disorder, in which individuals may eat objects that are not edible. Some examples include chalk, dust, plastic gloves (Yes!!!! I know what you're thinking, but there have been cases where individuals with ID have eaten plastic gloves), sponge bits, etc. This is a serious disorder and if it is not monitored properly, it could result in death of the individual because the item that was ingested may be huge or lethal.

Autism Spectrum Disorder: -

It is called Autism Spectrum, because the individuals that are affected are on the spectrum. They vary in terms ability, but one pervading factor is impaired social functioning. There are levels of severity in the DSMV, in terms of ability. The individual does not respond to social cues as a "non-autistic person" would. For example: They don't maintain eye contact; don't understand social expectations, etc.

Also, they engage in ritualistic behaviors, such as rocking, standing by a window in one spot, skin picking etc.

The individuals may be verbal or may have very limited verbal abilities.

It is called autism spectrum disorder because it is on a spectrum, varying between a lower and a higher level of functioning. There may be a very high level of ASD, in which the intellectual level of an individual is extremely high, but they are sorely lacking in social skills. The example that always comes to my mind is the fictional character of Sheldon Cooper from the "Big Bang Theory". A high level of autism spectrum disorder used to be called Asperger's Disease but is now on the Autism Spectrum.

"Sheldon Cooper from the Big Bang Theory" - a genius with extremely poor social skills - Possibly Autistic

For those of you who are not familiar with "Sheldon Cooper", there are speculations that Einstein may have had Autistic Spectrum Disorder. Again, he was a total genius, but may have been lacking in social skills. The treatment approach for ASD is Applied Behavioral Analysis (ABA), in which the individual is taught proper social skills using steps to acquire complete understanding.

Traumatic Disorders:

What is Trauma: Trauma is a hugely emotional reaction to a disturbing event/incident. When a person is traumatized, it means that the event created a lasting/emotional effect on his/her life. They may continue to react in a different way in response to trauma.

PTSD - Post Traumatic Stress Disorder; is usually associated with War Veterans, however, can occur with individuals who are victims of other traumatic events.

These individuals experience flashbacks (re-imagining the incident), nightmares, re-experiencing of incident. PTSD is assessed after a month of the incident.

Acute Stress Disorder: - This type of disorder occurs within 1 month of experiencing the disturbing incident.

Adjustment Disorder: A emotional reaction occurring in response to sudden situation.

"Didn't see it coming..."

For example: Moving from home to a college dorm... Usually occurring within 3 months of the incident.

War Veteran:

Commonly associated with PTSD

New College Student: Transitioning - Possible Adjustment Disorder

- You must have at least a working knowledge of the other diagnoses/disorders in the DSM, such as Eating Disorders, Gender Dysphasia, Impulse Disorders

Somatic Disorders:

What are Somatic Disorders? Somatic disorders have to do with physical reactions in response to psychological issues.

Conversion Disorder:

When an individual experiences pain, with no medical cause. (Extreme Example: An individual experiences temporary blindness)/paralysis

Factitious Disorder:

Falsifying symptoms in order to get attention. (**Think: Factitious - as Faking**)

Munchhausen's By Proxy:

A mental health problem that is made up by a family member; may lie about symptoms or manipulate medical exam results.

Malingering: Intentionally falsifying symptoms to achieve Personal Gain. (For example: Exaggerating symptoms in order to get Disability benefits.)

Impulse Control Disorders:

Just like it sounds, these are disorders that have with impaired impulses. Therefore, they may act without thinking, become aggressive and fly into rages.

Oppositional Defiant Disorder: - usually starts at 8; extremely angry, irritable; violates rules

Conduct Disorder: - also associated with children; children seriously violating rules and laws

Antisocial Disorder: - Adults; violates rules, laws; usually no remorse; Conduct Disorder can develop into Anti-Social Disorder

Neurocognitive Disorder: - Special Note: /Neurocognitive Disorder now replaces Alzheimer's Disease and Dementia; It is categorized by: Neurocognitive Disorder with Alzheimer's Disease

The difference between **Alzheimer's Disease and Dementia** is in duration and progression.

Alzheimer's Disease is a progressive disease, which indicates that it is slated to become worse.

Dementia is something that lasts a shorter period of time and is able of being medically treated.

It is difficult to list all the diagnoses/symptoms/disorders that are important for the Social Worker to know. For more extended information, consult the DSM V, which outlines the specific symptoms, duration and types of disorders.

Chapter 16

Short-term Therapies:

Gestalt

Gestalt therapy was formulated on Fritz Perls: Mainly, it focuses on the "here and now". It is a short-term therapy, which is more goal-directed and is a departure from more traditional types of therapy, such as Psychoanalysis.

Short-term therapies are considered more pragmatic, as they are more solution-based and don't require years of commitment for creating sustainable change.

Gestalt therapy is based on "gestalts" (parts of the self), some of which are darker parts

(Shadow) and some of which are brighter /figure - ground; These represent the parts of the self. (It can be likened to the concept of a "Dr. Jekyll/Mr.Hyde" understanding. Perls believed that each one of us has a dark, as a well a positive side. The individual is also given instruction to focus on "I" statements, such as "I feel neglected when you do...". This reduced the possibility of the other party feeling defensive.

Person-Centered Therapy:

Person centered therapy arises from the belief that every person has a self-actualizing tendency. Self-actualizing tendency is an inclination to grow/aspire to be more than a mere existing individual.

It is believed that through "unconditional positive regard" - acceptance, the individual will come to realize the self-actualizing tendency

Behavior Modification: Behavior Modification is used with kids with behavior problems and also individuals with Intellectual Disabilities. Because persons with ID are largely non-verbal and may communicate via maladaptive behaviors, it is important to find ways to attempt to control/modify their behavior. Some of the steps could include Verbal prompting (Prompting- reminders); Redirection (Re-orienting to another activity); Physical Interruption of the Activity (if it presents harm.) It also includes using Reinforcement strategies for positive behavior.

(SCIP- R) (Strategies for Crisis Intervention Prevention - revised) were developed to protect individuals with ID from self- harm and harm to others. These interventions can be thought of as self-defense mechanisms to secure protection. OPWDD (the governing body of individuals with Developmental Disabilities) is moving away from the model, however, they are still used in some IRA's. (Individualized Residential Alternatives); Replacement behaviors (substituting socially appropriate behaviors for maladaptive behaviors), Reinforcement strategies (rewarding positive behaviors), and etc.

ABA - Applied Behavioral Analysis is used with individuals diagnosed with Autistic Spectrum Disorder. It focuses on integrating and reinforcing individualized skills. The emphasis is on consistency and repetition. The individual should practice the skill consistently. Some possible skills may include: "Making eye contact"; "Following directions", "Taking turns when playing with others" (Socialization goals.)

Systems Theory:

This is a belief that a part of a system has an influence on the other parts of the system; (Ex. A family). It also speaks to the fact that the individual may be analyzed in terms of the system (s)he belongs to, such as the systems of family, culture, neighborhood, current political policies and etc. All of these influence the way an individual is impacted by these systems and in turn, how that person responds to and perceives reality.

Each family strives for a sense of harmony or homeostasis.

Boundaries: limits within a relationship. A boundary in a family could be enmeshed, meaning that the one member of the family is overly involved with the other.

Genograms: Maps of family relationships. It is a visual display of a family's relationships. A genogram is a useful tool to determine what the interaction/relationship is from one family member to another in a family system.

One of the examples of **Systems Theory is family therapy:**

Crisis Therapy: Crisis therapy came after tragedy of epic proportions, 9/11. The understanding of crisis therapy is it is a short-term, goal-directed and action focused approach. Some examples of Crisis therapy are: Post sexual assault; post hurricane/earthquake or a panic attack. Therefore, these matters going to be handled in a very different fashion than the traditional "helping process" approach. The Social Worker's primary responsibility to return the affected individual to a previous state of functioning - **homeostasis.** Rapport needs to be established quickly. There is no Assessment process required, since one knows the nature of the problem. After the individual returns back to his/her state of previous functioning, the S.W. will need to teach the individual adaptive coping techniques to adjust to the change that occurred. This is not long-term, continuous treatment and therefore, should be addressed in a quick, results-driven way.

Your answers on the exam should include Returning the individual back to the previous level of functioning/achieve homeostasis; teach coping mechanisms; establish rapport quickly; A crisis has a lifespan of 72 hours; treatment for a crisis lasts for about 4-6 weeks.

Family Therapies:

The focus of all family therapy is emphasized on the differentiation of family members within the family unit. It also focuses on the healthy boundary's development between family members.

In Family Therapy, the family is being treated as a whole.

The towering figure in Family Therapy is Bowen.

There are always roles in the family. Some examples are: **"The Family Hero"** - holds down the family; masks problems:

"The Scapegoat'/Identified Victim is someone who the family always places the blame on. Often, this family member gets into trouble or destructive situations.

The Caretaker: - The Caretaker takes care of everyone, except themselves.

The Mascot: tries to take away from the problems of the family by getting everyone to laugh.

The "This is Us" family members sometime struggle with being their own individuals, while also belonging to a family.

Strategic Family Therapy:

In this type of therapy, the social worker is the one that initiates what will happen during therapy. The presiding belief is that the family members are adaptable enough to fix the issues that are not working and formulate solutions to the existing problems.

Memory Tip: Think Strategic - SW initiates; Family members plan/strategize to fix

Structural Family Therapy: Memory Tip: Structures, hierarchies...

In this model, the SW joins the family in order to help resolve conflicts. The overall belief is that boundaries in family relationships are the most important to resolve in order to have an effective family system.

Bowenian Family Therapy:

The Bowenian approach focuses on a theory that improving the functioning of the whole family will have a positive impact on each individual member.

The following are the concepts that are associated with Bowenian Family Therapy:

Differentiation: - speaks to boundaries; the more separate/different a family member is, the healthier he/she will be as an individual and in relationship to the whole (family.)

Emotional fusion: - Just like in the term, fusion; the entire family experiences each other's emotions as a whole. If one individual attempt to individuate, it is perceived as a betrayal of the family.

An emotional triangle: A third family member is introduced into a two-people configuration. This serves to reduce anxiety throughout the whole interaction.

Family Projection Process: This is the process in which parents transmit their emotional problems onto the children. For example: A mother discusses her marital problems with the child.

Genogram: A genogram is a physical representation of a family tree. It displays detailed information regarding various relationships that exist within a family.

PRIMARY/SECONDARY AND TERTIARY PREVENTION STRATEGIES:

Primary Prevention:

Think: preventative; proactive: Examples: Putting up "Fire Safety" signs to prevent an incident; immunizing, safe sex practices...

Secondary Prevention:

This is a post-injury/incident prevention: Ex. Taking medicine for a certain condition.

Tertiary Prevention:

The focus here is managing long-term diseases. Some of the types of programs could be "Health Support groups" or "rehab programs.

Interpersonal Therapy: Interpersonal therapy is built on the notion that psychological problems are built on the dysfunctions in interpersonal relationships. It is mainly used to treat depression. It combines the techniques of CBT, as well as familial relationships to bring about awareness of how these interactions influence individuals' experience.

Chapter 17

Indirect Approaches in Social Work:

Indirect Practices are used in order to ensure services are delivered more effectively and efficiently. Thus, they are used to bring about changes in policies, programs or budgets.

-They don't involve personal contact with clients. They are usually performed with a committee, coalition or other group. An important part to comprehend about this practice is that you're still helping clients, however, you are helping them on a larger level.

Some examples of Activities of Indirect Practice are Policy Management (ex. pertaining to social service agencies) Program Evaluation (to monitor the effectiveness of programs), Administration (relating to social service agencies and how they conduct business practices and personnel issues) and Intervention with Communities (issues affecting communities, such as homelessness, sanitation, distribution of health care, etc.).

A **social policy:** is a rule that's been accepted by a legitimate authority and define what actions are allowed and what actions are prohibited. This can relate to political systems, service agencies, etc.

Social policy includes principles dictated by a society that guide how it intervenes in and regulates the relationships among individuals, groups, communities and social institutions.

Social Policy: includes plans and programs in education, health care, crime and corrections and also economic security.

Social policies may be influenced by **Collectivitism**: a push towards common good or **Individualism:** which place emphasize individual will and place more restrictions on individual liberty.

A shift to "**Macro**"/larger scale services grew out of the move to cities and the need for programs to be coordinated. Ex. In the 1900's, the first welfare department was created

Some examples of Existing Social Policies:

The Social Security Act of 1935: which arose out of the Great Depression and the realization that people could become poor due to some form of societal dysfunction. The Great Depression occurred in 1929 and resulted out of a Stock Market crash. Because of the societal nature of this phenomenon, a legislation grew to help the economic needs of the older, dependent, disabled and low-income population.

The Social Security Act of 1974 (revised Act) - started receiving through block grants from the federal government. A block grant is a system of disseminating funds that permit the recipient to determine how to best distribute the money. (Ex. The federal government distributing the funds to the states and allow them the freedom to disperse them as they see fit.)

Another example of a Social Policy is **Welfare Reform**: change in the welfare system. /Personal Responsibility and Work Opportunity Reconciliation Act (PRWORA). 1996. In the 1990's President Clinton amended the system for obtaining Public Assistance. It is no longer afforded to just low-income families, but includes a caveat, in which the recipients are required to work/participate in vocational classes in order to earn their welfare check. Secondly, there are time limitations on the time frame that the individual is entitled to benefits. For a family, the time frame is 5 years. For an individual, it is 2 years. **This change definitely affects low-income individuals (possibly our clientele and the society at large).**

ObamaCare: - The Patient Protection and Affordable Care Act of 2010 provided better access to health insurance and reduction in growth of health-care spending. In other words, persons that are not eligible for health insurance through their jobs and are not eligible for Medicaid are given the opportunity to buy their own insurance at a low-cost. This may also affect our clients are they are given more choices, as to how to obtain their health care.

The above-listed policies are not subject to automatic entitlement. Please see below the requirements by which benefits are determined.

Policies Affecting Social Service Delivery:

Eligibility for Services: Determination of which people may receive the help.

Exceptional Eligibility: is based on the sympathy vote for the group in question. (ex. War vets. There are more options for Veterans to receive benefits, at present.)

Selective Eligibility: Services or benefits are provided only to individuals who meet pre-established criteria. (Ex. Disability benefits, Public Assistance, Governmental Housing.)

Universal Eligibility: Services or benefits are provided in the same amount to all individuals in the nation.

Means Testing: - is a method used to evaluate a person's financial means or well-being. Ex. A person who has applied for disability may be asked questions about their finances, debts, health and number of dependents.

Categorically Need and Categorical Programs: Individuals who are automatically eligible for certain welfare benefits without a means test. Ex. Blind persons, elders, children without parents, etc.

Policy Practice in Social Work: involves efforts to influence the development, implementation, change, evaluations of social policies to ensure social justice to all. (Social Justice is one of our defining values as Social Workers.)

Needs Assessment: This is a system to identify nature, occurrence of a problem within a community. Its overall purpose is to assess the quality of existing services and resources for addressing certain conditions or problems and pinpoint the need for different services.

- One way of assessing the quality of existing services is through: Survey Research: Reviewing surveys of a target group, members and etc.; Gathering information and opinions by way of community forums, public hearings, interviews and focus groups; Collecting statistics (i.e., Utilization reports, Waiting lists, caseload data, etc.)

(Example): Unemployment rates could be an area of focus for a Needs Assessment.

Policy Management:

Steps:

Determine the policy problem (Evaluate its source); Implement the policy /Administrative or judicial or legislative directive - define at which level it will be implemented: Local, state or federal.

- **Inclusive Management Model:** A policy management approach which involves community participation.

- **Principal-agent model** emphasizes direct accountability in the policy to elected officials.

- **Expertise Model:** Emphasizes the application of professional judgment of behalf of the public.

- **Policy Analysis:** Used to evaluate a proposed or existing social policy.

Chapter 18

Macro Change Process in Social Work:

Macro-Level Interventions: are usually designed to improve the quality of life for clients, communities or employees in agencies.

Macro change efforts are ways to fulfil the commitment to the social justice value in the Code of Ethics. The effort is to promote greater social and economic justice to underserved, vulnerable or oppressed populations.

Systems involved in Macro Change Processes:

Initiator System: The initiator is the person or group that first recognizes the existence of a community or organizational problem.

A Change Agent:

A change agent is the individual who initiates the change process. The change Agent **System:** - This is the system that includes the change effort and a planning committee or task force that start to analyze the problem or the organization or community in which the targeted change will take place.

A client system is the individuals who will benefit from the change.

Support System: This is the system that includes individuals or groups that may be willing to support the change effort.

Controlling System is the individual or group with the power to approve the propose the change. Example of a Controlling System in an agency is the: Board of Directors.

Host/Implementing System: A host system is the organization with assigned responsibility for the area to be addressed by a proposed change/ (Includes the Employees and Volunteers who will have day-to-day responsibilities to implement the change.)

The target system is the individual, group, policy or practice that needs to be changed.

The action system is comprised of individuals from any or all of the other systems who have an active role in planning and implementing the intervention.

Application to Systems Theory in Macro Practice: - one part of the system will bring about changes in another part.

Approaches to Change in Macro Practice:

Policy Approach: A formal adopted statement that reflects goals and strategies on a course of action. (Ex. Policy regarding termination procedures in an agency.)

Program Approach: Sets of activities designed to achieve a set of goals and objects. Most programs are intended to provide services directly to clients or communities. For example.: Fund raining, public relations, etc.

Project Approach: Projects only exist for a limited period of time. A project may be developed to demonstrate a new intervention.

Personnel Approach: This approach addresses the way organizations, or their personnel go about doing their work.

The best way to Conceptualize Macro Change is to make it *COME ALIVE FOR YOURSELF!* Think of a policy/program/administrative approach that you would want to change if you had the chance.

Then, apply the *STEPS* to the *PROCEDURE:*

Steps in Macro Change:

1: **Analyze the problem/population/arena.** (Interview individuals affected by the problem/present data of findings)

2: **Develop the working hypothesis. (**How you think the problem came about).

3: **Develop working hypothesis for intervention.** (A tentative plan to solve the problem.)

4: **Select which approach you intend to change**: (policy, program, project, etc.)

5: **Build support for the change.** * (Coalition development may be important as there may be opposition in the change effort. /Coalitions: are alliance for a collective action. /ex. working teams) Stakeholders are individuals or groups that have a particular interest in the change, pro or anti issue. / Resource building in building support is also a key factor, as well.

6. **Estimate the probability for success.** / Formulating the objective clearly/ Force field Analysis: An assessment of significant factors that promote or inhibit change in a community or organization. /Determine relative strength of each driving force.

7. **Decide** whether or not to pursue the change effort.

8. **Select strategies to get the change approved.** (How to put the Change effort into effect:) (Collaboration: - used when a working relationship in which the action and target systems agree that change must occur.) / Support for resources is offered. / Example of Collaborations are: Creating task forces, conducting workshops, developing fact sheets, etc.

Capacity building: includes participation and empowerment. Participation refers to activities that involve members of the client system in the change effort. ("Putting a face to the issue" - it is one thing to hear about a defect with the system and is entirely a different thing to have someone discuss how they are affected by the flaw.)

Campaign: - used when the target system needs to be convinced of the importance of the change. /Also, impetus for allocating resources.

Co-optation: addresses the opposition by absorbing the target system members and other opponents into the action system.

Formal co-optation: leads to Coalition building. / Lobbying: amending the legislation; policy change. /Mass Media Appeal: Releasing stories to the media to influence public opinion. (Ex. Bringing a story onto your local television station to raise awareness and support for the change effort.) Contest: used when neither collaboration or campaign is possible due to disagreement or conflict. Contest tactics are aggressive!

Contest tactics include: /Bargaining and Negotiation:

Collective Action: involves pressuring tactics, such as picketing, sit-ins, meeting disruptions, boycotts.) Ex. Walking out on a job collectively in order to influence salary raises.

Class Action Lawsuit: - Suing an entity for a perceived violation of the law. The ruling of the court is expected to apply to an entire class of people.

9. **Plan the intervention.** (Goals and objectives/Measure the outcome.)

10. **Prepare to implement the intervention.** (Appoint leader; address logistical considerations, such as facilities, equipment and other resources.)/ Example: Recruitment of staff/ Development of job descriptions.

11. **Monitor the intervention.** (Data Collection.)

12. **Evaluate the effectiveness of the intervention.** (Evaluation Reports; Reports may be prepared for Stakeholders.)

Chapter 19

Social Agency Administration / Administration in Social Service Agency:

A Social Service agency: is an organization or facility that delivers social services under the direction and support of a Board of Directors and is staffed by Human Services personnel.

Social services: are activities carried out to help people solve problems (ex. health, etc.) **Institutional social services** are services that are provided by major public service systems *(Public agencies that administer financial services, housing assistance, etc.) A social service agency has a **Catchment area:** The geographic area in which all potential clients are served by a given agency.

- An agency also has a **Mission Statement**: - permanent description of the reasons why the agency exists.

A **Board of Directors**: preside over a private agency and has ultimate authority and responsibility of the agency's programmatic and financial operations.

Social Service agencies: - can be seen as open systems as they maintain themselves through the constant interaction with the external government. (For example: For purposes of funding or enlisting clients.)

Inputs: Inputs include resources: (funding, staff, facilities, clients)

Throughput: Services provided by the agency.

Outputs: The completion of a service to a client. The outcome of an existing service.

Administrative Objectives:

- Meeting organizational goals.

- Protecting the survival of the agency.

- Promote the growth of the organization.

- Communication of policies to the staff.

- Acquiring and allocating resources. (Ex. Fund-raising, political advocacy, grant writing.)

- Personnel and Staff Development: (Recruiting, selecting, educating staff.)

- Public Relations: (Representing the agency to the community.)

- Management: (Enforcing rules within the organization; /Forming task groups, committees.)

- Improving organizational effectiveness.

- Evaluation of organizational and staff performance.

The Role of the Agency's Board of Directors:

- **Policy Development** (Policies that guide the agency).

-**Program Development:** - Problem Analysis; Goals and objectives/Program and Service design; Data Collection.

- **Personnel:** (Hiring/firing Administrators.)

- **Gaining financial resources.**

-**Public relations;** (Developing relationships with key agency stakeholders.)

- **Accountability:** (Evaluation process of the program.)

Agency Policies: define the agency's mission and goals. (Structure of agency, job descriptions, rules, etc.)

Personnel policies: define the benefits, rights and responsibilities that the employer grants. /These are usually listed in the Policy and Procedures Manual.

- **How an agency is structured**: (Ex. Bureaucratic model). The bureaucratic system: allow substantial worker autonomy.

Revenue Sources: Block grants; Grants, etc.

Participatory Administration: is a method whereby staff are part of administration/involves democratic involvement in the development of agencies' policies and procedures.

Revenue Sources: are derived from governmental funds; donations, fees for services; fund-raising campaigns, investments. Ex. of a Fund-raising events: A party which is offered to key leaders, families, community members at a prescribed cost in order to raise funds for the clients/program/agency.

Block Grants: are lump-sum specific allocations that are left to local governments. Matching funds: Provide federal funds for each dollar spent by state-level agencies.

Grant Programs: Funds that are targeted towards a specific program. A grant may be used as a request for services. Often, in Social Services agencies, Administrators are responsible for writing a grant proposal. This document describes and outlines the agency and its clientele. It lists the types of benefits that are afforded to the client as a result of that agency. In turn, it requests funds in order for the development/continuation of the agency.

Cherry picking: - is a method of selecting only best-fitting, full paying clients and rejecting other clients that don't fit this standard.

Budgeting Methods:

Line-item budgeting: identifying expense categories and estimating the amount of money that would be needed to cover all expense for that specific category.

Functional Budgeting: identify expenses for each program and not the overall agency.

Zero-based budgeting: - beginning with no funds and justifying every expenditure and request for the coming year.

Program Development Stages:

Program development is undertaken in order to address a communal need. Some common needs in society may be Substance Use; Health Care measures; teenage pregnancy, crime prevention; mental health concerns and education. Community developers become involved in order to solve these problems by providing the recipients with services to target their problems.

Just like in other Macro Interventions, prior to developing a program, one needs to do a Needs Assessment. That is a formal evaluation of current services before creating different services.

Step 1: This is the preliminary stage of Program Development. At this point, the change agent may not know what to do with respecting to expanding the program. Therefore, they would need to check into other agencies in order to see their processes at work. Part of the needs assessment would include data review (for example, looking at hospital records to assess the rates of teenage pregnancy.)

Step 2: The third step is to develop goals and objectives. The goals would be Step 2: The second step is to create a planning committee. If this is conducted in an agency, it could include one person that is devoted to the effort or a small group of people that are involved to examine this issue dependent on the results obtained in the Needs Assessment.

Step 3 is to develop an Action Plan. This would include the Timeline of the project; the responsible parties and what the aim of the project is.

Step 4:   The 4th is to conduct a Literature review. A literature is review is important because it would show the efforts of previous projects and what things were effective and what things did not work. A literature review is similar to conducting research on a theory or a practice to see its benefits and its flaws. Literature reviews are done prior to developing new theories, studies and experiments. For ex. Try imagining Erikson developing his new Theory of Social Development. Before, he went into his own observations and beliefs of a theme of development, he studied other similar theories and observed inaccuracies in them and/ or added new information.

Also, if a student is writing his/her Ph.D. thesis, they will need to conduct a literature review (review of other publications, periodicals) to find out if the topic has been attempted before. Also, upon doing so, they will learn if the prior literature has flaws on the presented research and/ or needs further expansion. Based on the results of the literature review, the student will craft the thesis, with the original, as well as the previous information.

It is the same in a Literature Review for Program Development. Prior to suggesting ideas for improvement, a change agent must explore the methods and results in previous programs. It is also useful to do a Literature Review if you are unsure of the steps you are going to undertake for the Action Plan.

Step 5: Implementation of the Program: An important part of the implementation process is the trial period. In other words, the projected services in the program must be tested via a focus group or in an interview process. Once the pilot program has started, spreading awareness is important. It is necessary for new clientele to test the services and find out if they meet their needs.

Program Evaluation:

- Evaluating the efficacy of a program.

Criteria for Program Evaluation:

Effort (resources required to reach programmatic goals. Resources could include Staff, monies, etc.)

Impact; Effectiveness, Efficiency and Quality.

Program Evaluation Approach includes the

Quantitative Outcome Model (numbers/profit).

Qualitative Outcome Model (Clients' Feelings about the Program.)

(This is the part where some Research Methods are used.)

Program Evaluation Process:

Needs Assessment: Assessing the needs of target populations; an evaluation of existing services; An example of a Needs Assessment is Survey Research.

Formative Evaluation: - the gathering of information to determine the types of changes that are needed. Its purpose is to alter the program.

Summative Evaluation: The overall evaluation of the program's effects.

The Stages of Program Evaluation:

Stage 1: Planning phase (determining if the resources are sufficient enough to conduct the evaluation.)

Stage 2: Selecting a Research Design: - This is used to interpret data. (Ex. ABAB design, Quasi-experimental, Experimental, Single-Subject etc.)

Descriptive Survey Design: uses representative sampling and is used to elicit quantitative data that can be generalized to other participation. (Ex. Questionnaire, Interview process.)

Client Satisfaction Questionnaire: is used to solicit opinions regarding the services that were rendered. A Client Satisfaction Questionnaire may be presented to a client following the service. (For example, a clinical office may distribute a questionnaire to evaluate the level of satisfaction the client achieved with the program.)

Stage of 3 of Program Evaluation: is the collection and interpretation of data. Then, the results are applied for the purposes of altering the programs.

Staff Development:

Staff Development is necessary to improve client services. Staff development must be an internal agency procedure and also a community process.

Human Resources Plans:

- Predicting Personnel needs.

The roles of HR are to: Analyze jobs and create job descriptions from this analysis.; This is the basis of subsequent functions, such as Recruitment, Selection, Orientation, Supervision, Training, Performance Review and Termination Procedures.

Continuing Education is a crucial part of staff development. Continuing education inspires personnel and offers innovative and alternative ways for them to offer services to the clients.

Interorganizational Relations:

- Linkage to organizations is key to organization development.

Management: Administrators who are responsible to enforcing rules within an organization.

Autocratic Leaders: - make decisions independently.

Laissez-faire leader: - leave up decision-making to their subordinates.

Democratic Leaders: - Involve subordinates in decision-making.

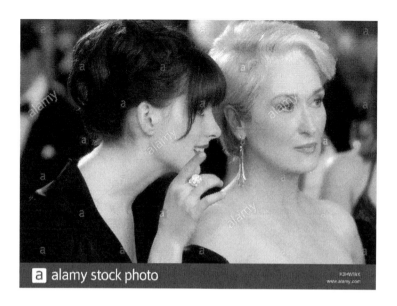

Guess what type of leader Miranda Priestley is? :)

Task Groups: A task force is a temporary group created to achieve a specific objective. Staff are encouraged to exchange information in this forum.

Planning Committee: This is also a type of short-term group targeted towards working on a certain project. However, the difference is that a Planning Committee is smaller than a task force would be. An example of a planning committee may consist of a program within your agency.

Conflict Resolution and Management Within the Agency:

One reason for Conflicts in an agency is differing roles of the domains (Policy, management and service.)

Policy Domain: individuals who have the authority to define the organization's mission, policies, etc. (Ex. Board of Directors.)

Management Domain: those individuals who ensure that an organization's policies are carried out. (Ex. Clinical Supervisor)

Service Domain: the individuals who are responsible for providing services to clients. (Social Worker.)

Strategies for Conflict Resolution: The Structural Approach: re-organizing work assignments; modifying procedures, addressing pay equality. When an administrator sees that the work is not distributed equally, it may result on unnecessary burden on some employees. Therefore, he/she will re-assign or delegate the work more evenly. Similarly, if there is unfair pay equality amongst the employees, the Administrator may advocate for raises for certain employees to make the salaries equitable.

Interpersonal Approaches: include Bargaining: Opposing sides exchanging offers within each other.

Mediation: A third party is brought in to use tactics to facilitate agreement.

Arbitration: Two sides are required to agree in advance to accept the arbitrator's settlement. (In voluntary bargaining: the conflicting parties only choose to accept the arbitration process, not the settlement.)]

The Information System: is the use of Information technology and activities that use the technology to support operations, management and decision-making.

Decision Support System: - involves using computers to collect and organize information and make decisions from indicated choices. The computer's decision is accepted.

Management Information System: (MIS): is used to acquire, process. analyze and disseminate data that are useful for carrying out organization-based goals.

- Its use may include Monitoring Staff Activit6y; Client services; Client Privacy and Client Services.

All these Macro systems including Service Delivery, Program Evaluation and Policy change are identified in order to improve the welfare and quality of lives for clients/individuals. Agency Personnel are included in these methods, as if the agency employees are uncomfortable, dissatisfied with their agencies, this sense of dissatisfaction is going to be disseminated to the clients.

Important Tip: Within a Macro Intervention, your role as a Social Worker is going to be active. For example, if your client may have been discriminated against and denied benefits, your task will be to help them fight for their benefits.

Chapter 20

Community Theory and Practices

Community Development and Organization has become a huge section on the ASWB exams, so I'm going to devote a lot of time on it. One of the main things to remember about Community Organizing and Development is that it is "Indirect Practice". Why is it indirect? Because the Social Worker works in tandem with the community, not for them. In other words, they partner with the community in order to effect improvement in community practices. Special Note: Community Process: is long-term.

What is a community? A community is a social system which is connected by a need for common goals.

Different Types of Communities:

Different types of communities can exist. For example, a community can, be bound by a geographical location (Town, neighborhood); A community can be defined by common interests, religion, sexual orientation.

The purposes of the community: These can be for the distribution of resources, such as food, clothing and shelter.

- **Social Control:** This is transmitted in a community by laws and the enforcement of law regulation.

- **Social Participation:** These offer a chance for community to express their interests and connect with one another: For example, a Church can be a community.

A church can also be a vehicle of support for vulnerable or needy members that need help.

Concepts in Community:

Linkages: These may be horizontal - within the community and the society at large:

Vertical: These connect communities to other existing communities.

Gemeinschaft: which is a German word that means community focuses the inter-connectedness of a community and their common bonds. This is a concept developed by Tonnie.

Gesellshaft: - In this model, people organize together to achieve a higher purpose; task-oriented.

A community functions as a social system in that it is delineated by boundaries, homeostasis (a state of harmony of equilibrium) and are bound by task-oriented functions. These functions could be the services that it offers or groups. Some of the services may include Police protection.

Anomie: - Anomie occurs when codes or values have become weakened in a community.

Community Practices adopt the principles of strengths perspective and resiliency, in that they identify the resources that the community has and the ability to solve problems. The **empowerment approach** assumes that communities can gain control over the decisions that affect them.

The Strengths perspective in community emphasizes the community's resources, other than limitations.

Power and Conflict:

Conflict theory: postulates that there is a natural hostility in a social system. In this model, individuals compete for resources, may be disqualified due to race or religion and are affected by the principles of power by presiding members.

There is definitely a linkage between community and political associations. A community is invariably affected by governmental laws, such as the federal or state government perspective on Public Assistance, for example.

Community Organization:

The emphasis here is on a collective effort to help individuals. These may exist at the local level (neighborhood or by interest groups.) It is also believed that a community may have a larger effect on social issues, than an individual on his own.

The Steps to Community Organizing:

1. **Assess the needs of the community/Determine the problem.** (In short, immerse yourself into the community in order to gauge the problem.) This method may be done by observation, surveys, needs assessments. You may also need to get to know key leaders in the community and develop relationships with them, so they could assist you in your goal. (Side note: If you read President Obama's autobiography - which I highly recommend - that is after you take this exam :), you will see that he was a Community Organizer as his steppingstone into political career.)

2- **Identify the needs/interests of the community.** These may not match your goals for them. For ex. "You think that a community needs a dog park. However, when the community members hear your proposal, which turn it down and say that they are not interested in a dog park. They need an after-school program. As you're working with the community, you need to respect their needs first. You also will not be able to get anywhere with your cause, without their support.

3 - **Analyze the problem**

4- **Developing a plan of action.** (What are you going to do to address the problem.)

5- **Recruit leaders in the community to contribute their efforts.** (This is a way to attract attention to your cause and gain more support in your effort.)

6- **Mobilize resources;** Identify the kind of resources that are already available in the community (funds, equipment, etc. This is what's known as a strengths perspective.)

The enabler: This is the type of Social Worker who brings individuals or organizations together to develop community groups.

Planner: The planner is in charge of providing means for service delivery.

Activitist: Advocacy for a certain policy/interest of the people.

The **Crux of Community Organizing** is to promote social justice, through proper funds allocation and other means of social well-being.

Social Planning: This is a long-term strategy to mobilize the community. Social planning involves the gathering of research, facts to sustain its efforts. (Ex. To eradicate the homelessness population.)

Social Action: Social Action is involved re-allocating resources. It is focused on targeting the oppressors (those with influencing power) in order to effect change. Often, negotiations are part of this process.

Who might the oppressors be? One example of an Oppressor may be a business owner or a building owner that may have an opposition to have a shelter for the homeless population in his business.

Another example of **an oppressor**: This is a real-life example for me. When I worked with the Intellectually Disabled population, there was a lot of opposition to having a group of our clients reside in a specified neighborhood. People were afraid; repulsed, uninformed as to what these types of clients represented. Some communities/neighborhoods did not want this population to be around them.

What would I do as a Social Activist? I would involve the oppressors (Co-optation) (in this case the people in the neighborhood) to educate them on people with Intellectual Disabilities. I would get them on my side and garner their support, so they see how important it is to integrate this special client population into their community. (This is a classic example of Community Organization). You are very likely to see this type of question on the exam and the answer is "Community Involvement". The key is always to partner with the community.

Locality Development: This involves the economic and social progress of the entire community, including the community's own resources. (Self-help options). Ex. Funds, community centers, food provisions, etc.

Community Development:

Community development is aimed at social justice. It may address areas such as mental health concerns, the economy, ecological issues and the like.

What could be an ecological concern? For example, a community may be interest in Wildlife Preservation.

Another example is **Climate Change/Global Warning.** I know that our current political leaders do not believe that this problem is occurring. However, evidence shows the effect of climate change over the last 10-20 years. Temperatures are increasing, the polar ice caps are melting, and animals are becoming extinct as a result of this huge phenomenon. As a Community Developer, you may want to look at "Global Warming" as a Community Development problem.

It has been said that Polar bears are at a risk of extension.

That truly saddens me! They are so very beautiful.

If our community is aimed as attempting to preserve the lives of Polar Bears, then that is Community Development.

What is an example of Mental Health Concerns?

This is also a nationwide problem. There have been numerous mass killings (in schools, synagogues, public recreational venues) at the hands of persons with mental disorders. How might you, as a Social Worker help? You, as a Community Developer would get involved to gather support for this national problem. Possible solutions may be: Mental Health Parity (equal medical procedures and medical insurance support for persons with mental disorders), more community awareness of mental disorders; gun control, more clinics for provision of treatments of these disorders.

Also:

- Improving communal resources

- Provide education opportunities

- Assist in self-sustaining options for the community.

- Political ties/involvement.

Community Developers enlist the help of the local community members for their support.

Community developers also assume the role of educator of the community.

Ex. Providing Sex Education or information on Diabetes Awareness.

Community Organization:

To key to remembering Community Organization is the focus on the word, **"Community"**. **Community Organization is a system whereby Social Worker help clients on a "Community level"**, not on an individual basis.

What happens in a community?

A community is used for socialization purposes, to express shared beliefs, such as attendances at a church. A community is also used to establish Control, in terms of regulations, laws, etc.

Purpose of Community Organization for Social Workers:

A community is aimed at common goals and objectives. In community organization or development, you are helping people in the community and not on an individual basis. In this type of social work practice, we, as the social worker work together with the community, not for them.

There are different types of Community Organization.

Locality Development: Working with the community to solve a common problem. Broker: The broker mediates between the community groups. He/She also negotiates between the group. / For example: Organizing a "Clean Up Day" to take care of the neighborhood's streets. Along with that, he/she provides linkages to community members to other services.

Social Planning: The Social Worker encounters a social/community problem and uses research to resolve the problems. Ex. Increased teen-age pregnancy in the community. Objective: Provide more Sex Education Information.

Social Action: In this role, the SW helps community members who require assistance. The Social Worker acts as an Advocate. / Social Action: - Think acting on behalf of the clients who needed services.

Social Reform: The Social Worker creates Reform by analyzing a common problem and bringing groups/agencies together to take action. For example: Lobbying for a new law; 2nd example: A social service organization is offering employees extremely low salaries due to increased costs. The SW in this situation will unite agencies/groups together in order to show the need for improved salaries for the staff.

Problem Solving Process Terms:

Counselor: A counselor may work on different tasks. She/he may help their clients identify their needs/. emotions; consider solutions for improvement.

Mediator: This role is executed when there is a dispute. In this case, the social worker will work to intervene between parties to help them settle their difference and come to agreements.

Macro-Level Advocacy:

This is a type of practice in which one works on behalf of the groups that are unable to advocate for themselves:

Cause Advocacy uses such as principles of operation as Persuasion: Convincing others to take a different position.

Fair Hearings: This is a process by which individuals who are denied benefits are entitled to be heard to obtain their fair treatment. Some examples may include Public Assistance Fair Hearings or other types of social services that involve the denial of entitlements.

The above is an illustration of Community Organization :)

Phases of Intervention:

We already spoke about the Client Process and the Social Workers' role in establishing a plan for meeting with the client. This section will focus on the level of interventions that the social workers will employ in each stage.

Micro Level:

At the micro level, the social worker's role is to help clients solve their own difficulties.

Mezzo Level: The second level of intervention is referring to large communities or groups of people. At this level, social workers try to make connections between the Micro and Macro level.

Macro Level: This level deals with the economic, environmental, socio-economic and other influences that are affecting the client. The role of the social worker is to try to eliminate barriers to the economic, medical barriers that may be preventing the client to achieve a well-established life. Usually, this is within the community or at organization work.

 For example: If a social worker works in a disability/public assistance office and their client tells them that they are unable to work, the social worker's duty is to find the tools to empower the client, so they are able to work.

Change Agent: A change agent is part of a group to works to improve some part of service delivery. The change agent analyzes the problem, population affected, community and etc. The change agent is the initial steering committee, until a more organizations get involved. A change agent is involved at the Macro Level of the process.

What type of Change Does Macro Practice Effect?

It is mainly directed at Policies and Practices: That is why you usually receive a "Policy and Practices Manual" when you first start working at an organization.

- Social Policy

- Programs

- Specified projects

- Employee conflicts

Chapter 21

Research:

Even though this is a small part of the AWSB Exam, I would like to include some basic concepts to de-mystify the subject of research. I find that many social workers have a problem in this area, and I am here to break it down, so people can easily understand the role of it when it applies to Social Work. Also, some Social Workers may be thrown off by the term "Research" as it pertains to Social Work. So, what does Research mean in our field? Research in the general sense is the collection of information. It is applicable to Social Work, mainly in the form of Evaluation. We have discussed Program Evaluation in the Chapters relating to Macro Change. Some of the research principles we will use will refer to Program Evaluation.

Purposes of Research:

1. Research is used to monitor the effectiveness of an agency, client intervention, process.

For example: The Social Worker Supervisor implemented a system, in which his supervisees implemented the use of the "Beck Depression Inventory" prior to treating clients with depression. The SW Supervisor wants to see if this Inventory was useful in helping treat the depressed client.

Example 2: An administrator wants to evaluate the progress a treatment center made, in terms of their effect on the client population and their staff productivity.

Example 3: I want to see how well my book/tutoring services prepared SW students for their exam.

It is for the above-following reasons and many other situations in which Research will be useful.

When experimenters/social workers/ administrators set out to analyze the way a system works or its effectiveness, they may create studies, experiments, quizzes, designs to test out a system.

The building block of the Research Model is the Independent Variable and the Dependent Variable relationship. If you understand this relationship, this will set the stage for understanding further research concepts.

The independent variable: - the variable that has the effect on the **Dependent variable.**

Dependent Variable - the outcome.

Purposes of Statistics:

Ah, those dreaded statistics. Many people don't like statistics and don't know why statistics are necessary in Social Work.

If we go back to the 1st example, say the SW Supervisor used 75 clients in his study to evaluate the use of the "Beck Depression". It would be extremely difficult and time-consuming to test every client in the study. Therefore, statistics are used. For example: The Supervisor may want to use an "average" for all of the clients as a pointer for his results. **Mean -** refers to the average. Other terms that may be used are Mode **-** the number that occurs most often on a set of data.

Median: - the point between the starting point and the ending point; think of it as the Center. (Middle point.)

The mean, median and Mode are applicable when having to do with Shapes of Distribution. When we talk about Shapes of distribution, we are discussing the ways research is visually plotted on the graph.

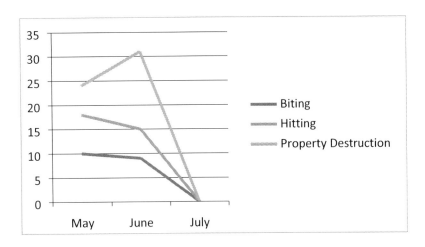

This is a simple graph to illustrate the distribution of a set of maladaptive behaviors for a 3-month period. The ways the line is positioned reflect the "Shapes of Distribution" depicted in the graph. The Distribution that's shaped like a bell is considered to be a normal distribution. Positively skewed distributions: The positive line is extended

Negatively skewed distributions: The negative tails are extended; Most of the information is located in the positive side of the distribution.

Accuracy:

Accuracy is instrumental in Research. You want your study/experiment to be accurate, as you want to gauge the truest relationship that occurs between the Independent and Dependent variable. There are several methods to account for Accuracy. One way is to assess its Reliability: Reliability refers to generalizability to other populations/circumstances.

Research designs are in fact evaluated by their **Reliability - Method of Understanding**

Reliability: - Reliability in research is just like it sounds. Is the instrument, study, research design reliable? In other words, if you use it a year from now, will it still yield the same results?

Are the results being consistent across time. Ex. Many people will relate to this one. If you're trying to lose weight and weigh yourself throughout a few times during the day and you get LARGELY different results (without significant input of food); The reliability of the Scale is not good! It means that the instrument (the scale) is ineffective in achieving reliability on your actual weight.

and Validity - if the experiment measures what it is intended to measure. **Method of Understanding**: - is the instrument, design, study valid?

For example: If you use the same scale that we used for Reliability; is the scale accurate? If it is way off in measuring someone's weight, then it is not valid and it does not matter that it has reliability. Validity has to come first.

Another Ex. If you're using a thermometer and it doesn't give you the accurate measurement, then it's not effective.

Internal Validity: Assesses whether or not there is a relationship between the ind. variable and the dependent variable. It also looks at whether or not that relationship has a cause and effect.

External Validity: This method assesses whether or not the relationship between the Independent and Dependent Variable generalizable to other settings?

Some Examples of External Variables that exist:

- Maturation

- Fatigue

- The rater may be more experienced during the post-test than in the pre-test

- The precision or lack thereof of devices

- Subjects dropping out.

Threats to External Validity:

- Reactivity: The notion that subjects are observed may skew their performance.

- Hawthorne Effect: The tendency for subjects to perform better under observation.

- Interaction between testing and treatment.

- The nature of the study itself.

- Demand Characteristics: Knowing the nature of the study.

All of these factors may influence the validity of the study being performed.

In a single-blind technique: subjects are not told about the nature of the experiment in order to control Reactivity. In a double-blind technique, neither the researcher nor the subject is told about the nature of the experiment.

Ways of Measurement:

Because researchers want to achieve validity and reliability in your experiment/study, they set up different designs to test out those experiments.

The data collected may also be represented on different graphs:

For example: When I used to work with Individuals with Intellectual Disabilities, I would collect data on the types of behaviors they had throughout the months. (Note: Behaviors were sometimes used as forms of communication, as most of my client couldn't speak.) After I collected the data, I would use it to compare how an individual did from one month to the next. Based on that, I would see if I would need to change the Behavior Treatment Plan and/or medications. Note: I used the above-mentioned graph to represent the similar type of data:

Refer to the below Graph:

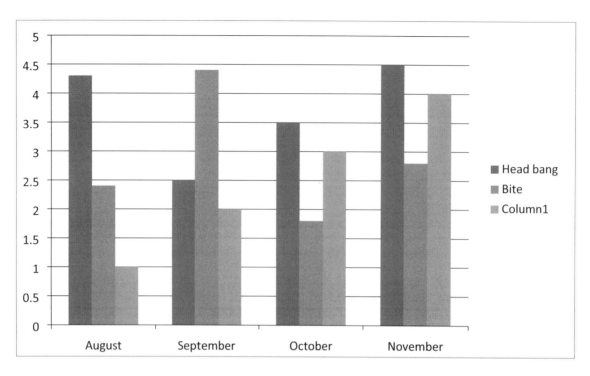

From this chart, you can see the Mode: (The number that appears the most is 4.5; therefore, it is the Mode; The approximate average or mean for "Head banging behavior " is 3); The median is not easily discernible, as this is a table and there is not linear distribution.

Scales of Measurement:

Descriptive Statistics: are used to describe and summarize data; Inferential Statistics: are used to draw conclusions about the relationships between the Independent and the Dependent Variable.

Nominal Scale: A nominal scales divides variables in unordered categories: For ex., Sex, Eye color, Political Affiliation.

Ordinal Scale: An Ordinal Scale is one that you may have seen many times. It divides observations into categories and also provides information on the order of the categories: It is your famous Likert Scale that may have the following options: 1 - Strongly Agree; 5 - Strongly disagree and anything in between those two categories.

Interval Scale: This is exactly as it sounds. It is based on intervals based on measurement scales. For ex.; Temperature scale.

Ratio Scale: A ratio has properties of order, equal intervals and an Absolute Zero Point.

How Research Designs are formulated:

Group Samples:

Group samples are selected in order to proceed with a study or an experiment. They also exist as a tool for comparison between groups.

A research design must include the client population group and the process of selection of this population. For example: "Persons that have been depressed for a 5-year period"; "Another example: "People that took the ASWB Exam and did not pass it".

The sample group must be reflective of the population and the population's characteristics.

Simple random sampling: Every part of the sample has a chance of being included.; (Reduces favoritism, bias...)

Stratified sampling: Each "Strata" - population trait is included in that sample. To avoid confusion, you must separate the sample group into separate categories, as grouped by education level, age, ethnic background, etc.

Control Group: The group that does not receive the intervention; This group is used as a source of comparison. (Study Tip: C - Control / C for comparison; E - Experimental - the one that receives the experiment.)

Experimental Group: This is the group that receives the intervention.

Experimental Research: This type of research is used specifically to test out the beliefs about the influences of 1 or more independent variables on dependent variables. This type of research is also concerned with accuracy. Therefore, it uses techniques to eliminate external influences that may exist, besides the Independent and Dependent Variable.

True Experimental Research: is designed to see if the control/intervention in the independent variable indeed affected the dependent variable.

Quasi-Experimental Research: This also concerns the interest in whether or not the independent variable caused a difference on the dependent variable. However, in this type of research, the subjects were not randomly selected, so therefore it is not always easy to ascertain whether there was indeed a correlation (relationship) between an independent variable and dependent variable. Reasons for no random selection: No volunteers were available; etc.

Developmental Research:

This is a very interesting type of research. This research serves to examine the changes that occur in a person during the passage of time. These changes could include Social Development, psychological development, physical maturation and Age.

Longitudinal Studies: (Memory Tip: Think - long....); Longitudinal Studies assess a specified group of people over long periods of time. Ex. The medication effects of Prozac on a selected group over the period of 5 years.

Cross-Sectional Studies: This is an evaluation design, in which groups of people are observed at different stages at the same point in time or at different ages.

Cross-Sequential Design: This design focuses on assessing members of two or more age groups at 2 different times.

Group Designs:

This is used to assess one or more groups of subjects.

Single Subject Design: This is used to research the influences of the independent variable on one subject or a very small group of subjects.; In a Single-Subject Design, there is no Control group. The group that is studied is its own control group. One example that may be used is a Single-Subject Design is the best type of research practice in a psychiatric facility. The reason for that is because there is only one group of people being studied.

Multi-group Design: - involves one or more group of subjects.

Qualitative - analyzing content of the material /not numbers; definitions, traits, etc. Ex. A mood diary.

Quantitative - analyzing numbers; Data (An example of Quantitative Data Analysis may be my above-pictured graph. I can use that graph to analyze the number of behaviors that an individual displayed over a certain number of months.

To reiterate:

Dependent Variable: - the variable that changes as a result of the independent variable

Ex. Independent Variable - "Sugar pill given to subjects"

Dependent Variable: - Change in their behavior as a result of the pill.

The AB Design: The AB design is the pre-test; post-test. X is measured before the intervention (pre-test); (Baseline) and then is measured after the intervention (the post-test).; A Baseline could be: "A person's usual mood"; The intervention is the - medication.

ABAB design: The baseline (prior to treatment/intervention) (A) is followed by treatment/intervention (B); then A is taken away and B - reintroduced; An easier way to understand the ABAB design is different stages of intervention/treatment. You may also think of it as "More than one baseline" for the design. This design is developed to test out the effectiveness of the intervention.

ANOVA Test: - analyzing different group means within a sample. This is used in hypotheses testing.

Chi-Square: How well the distribution of data fits with the distribution if the independent variables were independent. This is a statistical method to assess the goodness of fit between observed values and those that are expected theoretically.

Research is important in evaluating programs, methods, treatments, etc. Therefore, it is included in the Social Work core program and the Exams. A social Worker may use data in his work on a daily basis and not necessarily realize it. For example, if a Clinical Social Worker has designed a goal for his client to become less depressed in a period of 6 months, that goal must be measurable. It is important to assess progress, as well as for billing purposes. A SW may design a Treatment plan to states:

"Mr. X will show less depressive mood by going out and socializing on a weekly basis for a period of 3 months." This is a sample; Mood/Behavior Treatment Goal.

Standard Deviation: A Quantity calculated to indicate the extent of the deviation for a group as a whole

Hypothesis Testing:

This refers to other methods to assess the existence of a relationship between the Independent and the Dependent Variable.

Null Hypothesis: This is concept that implies there is not relationship between the Independent and the Dependent Variable. In most of your answers, you will want to Reject the Null Hypothesis because if you're conducting Research, you want there to be a relationship between the Independent and the Dependent Variable.

Alternative Hypothesis: - shows that there is a relationship between the Independent and the Dependent Variable.

Type I: - This is when the null hypothesis is rejected.

Type II: - This occurs when you retain a false null hypothesis.

These goals are important to assess the efficacy of treatment interventions in Social Work. They also used for insurance purposes to prove the necessity for further treatment. In short-term therapy models, a client may be only billable for a period of 6 weeks. If he desires further treatment, it must be supported by his diagnosis and a treatment plan that includes goals and objectives.

I hope that cleared up any misunderstandings on Research, Research Design and Statistics and I hope you realize why Research is useful and important.

Chapter 22

Psychotropic/Psychoactive Medications

Part of the assessment process is having, at least a working knowledge of the types of medications that the clients are taking. Therefore, it is important to familiarize yourself with some of the most common psychotropic medications. Medications are also covered on the exam.

The truth of the matter is that there is a myriad of medications having to do with psychiatric disorders and emotional challenges. One of the reasons that there are so many medications is because when a medication is first introduced, it is usually reported as having little or no side effects. However, as more and more people begin to take the medication, they start reporting more and/or different side effects. This usually leads to a dissatisfaction with the medication and a desire for a new one.

The Social Worker needs to have at least a working knowledge of medications. It is important, since they will be reading medical records, psychological testing reports and other pertinent information relating to the type of medication that the client is taking. The Social Worker needs to be knowledgeable with the medication and its uses. This is important so he/she could assess whether the medication is treating the right diagnosis/problem behavior/emotional state. Also, many clients come in with a starting dose of a medication or a change in medication or a longevity with a certain type of medication. It is crucial to know how the individual is responding to the medication at different points in the time frame they are taking it. It is also necessary to ascertain the condition of the client, as based on the medication he/she may be taking. For example, if the client is observed to have significant changes in cognitive or emotional functioning, it is important to evaluate the efficacy of the medication and/or possible non-compliance in adhering to the medication regimen. If there is suspicion that the medication is not working (as based on the symptoms the client may be having), a psychiatric evaluation needs to be recommended. It is important to note that Social Worker cannot force clients to take the medication, but the situation needs to be examined (**via an exploration/discussion**) to guide them in making the appropriate decision.

Clients may also have different side effects to the new or existing medication they are taking. There may be an adjustment process to taking a new medication or a withdrawal process, when being weaned off it. Social Workers need to be aware that the clients' responses/reactions during treatment/services may be influenced by the above-mentioned factors.

Some questions on the exam will ask you how the medications work, and some will be recall questions, in which you will be expected to know the generic and the trade name of a certain medication.

Here is a quick guide:

Anti-depressants: Anti-depressants act on the neurotransmitters: Serotonin, Dopamine and Neuroepinephine.

A quick way to remember trade names of the anti-depressants is that many of them end with a "tine"

Prozac -   Fluoxetine

Paxil   -   Paroxetine

Sertraline -   Zoloft

Effexor -   Venlflaxine

Celexa -   Citalo

Lexapro   -   Escitalopram

Wellbutrin -   Buproprion

Anti-anxiety medications:

A quick way to remember anti-anxiety medications is that many of them end in "zepam".

Klonopin   -   Klonozepam

Valium   -   Diazepam

Ativan   -   Lorazepam

Buspar   -   Buspar

Xanax -   Alprazolam

Bipolar Disorder Medications:

Lithium - Lithium is the medication that's most known for treating bipolar disorder. An important factor to remember with Lithium is that when an individual takes Lithium, their blood levels need to be checked regularly. It needs to be checked to assess for possible toxicity.

Tegretol   -   Carbamazepine

Topamax   -   Topiramate

Depakote -   Diavalproez

Anti-Psychotics:

Risperidal

Thorazine

Haldol

Invega

Abilify

Ayprexa

Psychostimulants: (For treatment of ADHD:)

Ritalin -   Methulophenidate

Adderal -   Amphetamine

Concerta

Dexedrine

Strattera

Medications used to treat symptoms of Substance Use Addictions:

For Heroin: Suboxone and Methadone

For Alcohol: Antabuse - this is an aversive technique to cause nausea to the scent of alcohol.

Vivitrol/Naltrexone (Generic/Brand) - is used to take away cravings of alcohol.

For Opiates: Vivitrol /Naltrexone

SSRI's - used to treat depression disorders; Mode of Action: (the way they work) - is by enhancing the functioning of nerve cells in the regulate emotion (Affected neurotransmitter: is Serotonin)

MAOI's - extremely strong antidepressants; they work on preventing the breakdown of Serotonin, Dopamine and Norepinephrine.

You may be asking yourself why there are so many medications. In the 20th Century, there were virtually no medications to treat psychiatric disorders. Thorazine was largely used and there were no other options. In the 21 Century, more and more medications started to pop up. The reason is that is that the previous medications were reported to have significant side effects. Every time a new medication is introduced, it is usually reported to have very little side effects. However, as the patients begin taking them, they tend to start reporting more side effects. Therefore, more medications are being made, to have as little side effects as possible.

Tardive Dyskenesia: TD is a phenomenon that occurs when an individual has been taking anti-psychotics for a very long time and start developing very serious side effects. Some of the side effects may be a protruding tongue and jerky/uncontrollable movements.

Cogentin is the medication that is widely used in conjunction with anti-psychotic medications in order to take away the side effects of the anti-psychotics.

Chapter 23

Substance Use

Substance use and abuse is a presiding problem within the client populations you will be working with, so we need to devote a special section to Substance Abuse/Chemical Dependency.

Alcohol: Alcohol is used as a relaxant and is a depressant.

If it is used in moderation and there is no family history of alcohol dependence or abuse, it's safe, if done socially and occasionally. However, Alcohol addiction is built on a DISEASE MODEL! The abuse of alcohol has the most potential to be lethal, out of all the other substances. It needs to be treated accordingly.

When we think of withdrawal effects, think of the opposite:

Alcohol Withdrawal Effects include Tremors and seizures; So, if you abuse alcohol for relaxation or as a lack of inhibitions, you will encounter the opposite if you stop taking it: Tremors and seizures.

Cocaine Addiction: Cocaine is used as an upper; the user may be up for days, energetic/nervous; restless and also lacking appetite.

Cocaine Withdrawal: - the opposite: That includes fatigue, nausea and vomiting. The user may experience 3 restless nights, for example and then crash and sleep for 3 days.

Cocaine Addiction is serious and shouldn't be overlooked. Many of our favorite celebrities and other people in the Creative Arts have abused and became dependent on cocaine. **One example** is the great singer, 'Whitney Houston", who unfortunately couldn't manage her drug use and ended up passing away at a very tender age.

Whitney Houston was also one of my all-time favorite singers. She fell into cocaine addiction and couldn't beat it. The result was tragic!

Heroin Addiction: Heroin is the most addictive Substance. Heroin addicts require treatment and are likely to die if they do not receive treatment and/or stop using.

Heroin gives the user a "calm high", a feeling of Euphoria.

Heroin Withdrawal Effects: The opposite of the Heroin use is when the substance is withdrawn and the user feels anxious, restless and has bone pain and muscle spasms.

Heroin is treated by Methadone and Suboxone.

A special Section should be dedicated to Opiate Addiction: This is a fairly recent epidemic, but it is serious and can be extremely dangerous and lethal to the person that may be using/abusing it.

Opiates are painkillers and narcotics (sedatives). They are used to treat pain. These substances are particularly harmful because they can be easy to get. An opiate can be prescribed as a post-operative treatment. It may also be given to a family member for a medical condition. If an individual resides with that family member, it will be highly accessible and therefore will serve as a danger to the person that has not received the prescription.

The opposite of Opiate Use/Withdrawal Effect is Restlessness, sweating, diarrhea, nausea, vomiting and dilated or watery pupils. Opiates are very strong medications and should only be taken as prescribed.

The great musician, Prince Rogers Nelson died from opiate addiction. He sustained two hip surgeries in his lifetime, after which he was prescribed Opiates. He became addicted to the Opiates and took a very dangerous one, called Fentanyl. Fentanyl is extremely strong and could stop the heart from beating, if taken in improper amounts. Prince overused the substance and was found dead in his home "Paisley Park" on April 21, 2016.

(The following images were taken by me, in Princes's hometown of Minneapolis, Minnesota. The first one depicts Paisley Park - his home/studio and the second one was taken on the gate of the "Paisley Park" home. I, like many other devastated fans went to Minneapolis to hear the Revolution after Prince passed away!)

This is Paisley Park! It lights up in purple every night! :(

First Lady, Melania Trump has started a campaign on Opiate Addiction, which definitely warrants our attention!

More Substance Addictions Definitions:

Substance Dependence: - is characterized by the presence of Tolerance - needing more and more of the substance to get the same "high" and Withdrawal - meaning when one stops the substance use, withdrawal effects are present (i.e., tremors, nausea etc.)

Substance Abuse - is the excessive use of the substance. It may not interfere with someone's full overall functioning; however, it is an increased use of the substance which may lead to other complications (Substance dependency, medical disorders, etc.)

Thus, Substance Dependence is more serious.

The most likely relapse time frame after substance rehab programs is within 1 year.

It is generally advised and enforced that the persons with substance abuse problems do not associate with the same social group that they were involved before (ex. a group of drinkers, coke users), so as not to interfere with their recovery process.

Working with the SU population:

If working as a **Drug Counselor**, the affected individual must want to get help. As a social worker, your job will be to break through the denial of the Substance User and support him/her once the user is ready to accept the addiction. Substance Use Counselors also introduce other coping methods to sustain change.

With Substance use, co-occurring conditions are common. (Co-occurring - mental illness and chemical dependency; MICA). If co-occurring conditions exist, the counselor must ascertain if the substance use resulted in a mental disorder or whether or not the mental disorder predisposed the individual to start using. Often, it is a combination of both. Therefore, a thorough Assessment is necessary.

Research shows that there are hereditary factors associated with the use of substances. However, cultural and peer expectations may also be the norm. If a person is "ego - dystonic" (needing to use defense mechanisms to cope with reality), he/she may resort to Substance use. Substance Use also becomes a way to cover up uncomfortable feelings, events and behaviors. It is crucial to work with persons on areas of self-esteem. It is also necessary to forge and encourage a social lifestyle. When Substance Users socialize with other substance users, it is difficult to stop.

When working with this population, the Social Worker will go through the helping process in a similar way. They will establish rapport, complete Assessments/ provide referrals (ex. methadone clinics, A.A., rehab develop treatment plans (which measure treatment goals), evaluate the progress provide support during treatment and post-treatment) and terminate.

Rehab clinics provide many services, including "Safe detox", while on medical supervision, Assessment, Counseling, Groups Sessions and Follow-Up in a Therapeutic Community. (TC). TC's are "patient-centered medical health for providing ongoing recovery support. Substances, such as "Antabuse" may be used. Antabuse is an aversive technique, in which the individual becomes nauseous to the smell of alcohol.

Most rehab facilities do not allow for outside intervention (families, friends).

This means that families and loved ones are not allowed to visit. The reason for that is that the afflicted person cannot be influenced by outside sources. They are prevented from reading books, (an outside influence) and are encouraged to focus solely on the program. The person can check him/herself out of voluntarily. However, it is strongly recommended to stay for the duration of treatment. Once the person has completed rehab, the rehab treatment team helps him/her with the adjustment to living independently (out-patient treatment, housing, family support).

The A.A./N.A. Model is founded on 10-step/ spiritual approach. The individuals subscribe to methods, such "accepting things they cannot change", "asking forgiveness from other people for the effect that the substance use has produced and etc. It is also based on group sharing. Sponsorship is an option. It is a voluntary treatment option but the structure of open-ended groups, as well as closed-ended groups are possible.

Chapter 24

Different Practice Settings:

As a Social Worker, you may be hired to worked in many different practice settings. Some of these settings are hospitals, clinics, schools, prisons and hospices.

It is important for you to know what is expected in some of these situations. This section is particularly useful for the LCSW Exam, as more focus is placed on working in different practice environments.

Overall, the key to working in different practice settings is using direct observation. It is important to form your own impressions of the client(s), rather than depend primarily on previous information. Chart reviews may be used to examine the background history of the client. Once you become familiar with the client, the "helping process" will be applied. (Rapport, assessment, etc.)

Prisons/Jails:

As a social worker in a correctional facility, you may be faced with multiple different situations. For example, you may be working with individuals with Substance Use issues, mental disorders, gang affiliations. You may be involved in groups discussing Anger Management or groups targeted towards educational aspirations.

As a general rule, Social Workers support Rehabilitation upon re-entry into the larger society, rather than the "Retributive Approach. The "retributive approach" focuses on the punitive aspect of crime control. (Retribution for the crime). However, Rehabilitation Model" emphasizes the corrective aspect of crime prevention and control. This would indicate that we do not use punitive measures and believe in the reformation of a client's character. Therefore, your major focus would be assisting clients upon re-entry into society.

As a result, the issues you may face will be associated with clients' re-entry into the free world. He/she may have been released, but there is still a "so-called label on him/her" that says "Convict". This may limit his/her choices and possibilities, as far as attaining work, education programs, housing, etc.

Another common occurrence is the lack of resources as associated with ex prisoners' reality. The prisoner may not have worked in a long time. He/she doesn't have many opportunities with respect to employment and financial options. Usually, many people don't want to hire someone with a record. It therefore results in a vicious cycle. One of your tasks may be to help the former convict identify resources, housing options, employment opportunities, etc. This is imminent as the lack of these provisions may result in further crimes, such as theft and a probably return to prison. This notion is referred to as "Recidivism". (The likelihood of a prisoner to re-offend.) The client may also become accustomed to the "prison existence" (such as in "Shawshank Redemption") and may find it difficult to return to outside society. The Social Worker's goal in this instance would be to identify the benefits for the ex-prisoner to live in the external world.

Another aspect affiliated with prison culture is the notion of "lack of disclosure". For example: As a new inmate enters the prison system, he/she may be tempted to ask others what crimes they committed. If you watch any prison movies, the answer will usually be "Don't ask any questions", or "No snitching", "Keep to yourself" and "Mind your own business". Therefore, the prison culture fosters an emphasis on a lack of shared information amongst inmates. This makes it particularly difficult for a Social Worker to conduct any groups, since they require exposure to relevant information. A possible question on the exam may have to do with prison culture. Your choice should reflect the custom of privacy amongst prisoners.

If you're treating an involuntary client, resistance is natural. Your technique would be to validate the resistance and offer ways of how you can help as long as the client has no choice but to attend sessions.

The Educational System:

Social Workers often find themselves working in schools, such as charter schools, special educations programs, and etc. Regardless of the type of school it is, the issues will be very similar. Some of the difficulties the clients may experience are behavioral difficulties, educational problems, family concerns, bullying, gang affiliations and abuse/neglect issues. The solutions to these problems are as varied as the problems themselves.

For example, in the cases of gang affiliation, students may join gangs for a sense of belonging and in order to avoid being harassed.

Bullying is defined as when an individual asserts his/her authority/right over a less threatening individual. In the case of bullying, several laws under the Title IX of the Civil Rights Act prevent school officials from being able to avoid the issue of bullying.

Your Role as a School Social Worker and How this may appear on the Exam:

Common Issues in School Social Work situations:

- Your first step when a child is referred to you will be to speak to the child. Based upon the child's responses, you may need to contact the parents to obtain more information.

- In cases of suspected abuse, you will follow the same protocol as in other abuse situations: If you have reason to believe that abuse/neglect has occurred, you need to notify the authorities.

- If a child has occasional bruises, marks, scratches, you need to gain more information. The reason is that this may be a developmentally appropriate occurrence. For example, if a child is on a sports team, it is natural that he/she would show bruises on occasion, as a result of the sports activity.

- In order to address bullying, you would need to focus on adaptive mechanisms to help the victim cope with the consequences of bullying behavior. On a community-wide scale, you may want to join anti-bullying campaigns and raise awareness on the epidemic of bullying.

- For gang affiliation, the need to emphasize the role of family is important. The most prominent reason why individuals join gangs are to gain a sense of family and unity. The roles of substance use and mental health may also be addressed because they may be other presenting factors of why the individual wants to join the gang.

- If a child demonstrates a change in ability (ex. a sudden onset of hyperactivity, frustration, lack of concentration and concentration); a Physical and a subsequent psychological evaluation is required. This may be indicative of a learning disability, ADHD, or etc.

If you're working in a different facility (not a school setting) and require information from a teacher, you need to ask for a consent release form (from the parent) to be able to speak to the teacher.

Other School Social Work Concerns:

It is also important to note that **F.E.R.P.A.** is a big part of the school system process.

F.E.R.P.A. refers to the **Family Education Rights Privacy Act.** The FERPA states that all school records are confidential and are the sole possession of the school. However, all documents pertaining to students are accessible to parents. Moreover, all parents have the right to change information that they deem to be inaccurate regarding the records. I think this part make sense as sometimes school officials have a tendency to make mistakes on the child's information. How This May Appear on the Exam: If the question states whether or not the parents have the right to alter children's records, the answer is "yes."

Another situation you may come across is the proper placement of students with disabilities. This procedure is addressed similarly to other problem-solving methods in the social work system. The system is based on the following steps:

R. - Review of charts/student records.

I. - Interventions

O.- Observation

T. - Test

Once this procedure is implemented, the treatment team devises an **I.E.P. (Individualized Educational Program)** that is composed of measurable goals and objectives, which target academic and functional needs. The I.E.P. must be reviewed on an annual basis. It must also be re-written every 3 years.

When considering options of placing a child with disabilities in a residential setting, the Social Worker must ensure to place that person in the least restrictive setting. Least restrictive implies - as much as independence as possible, based on their level of functioning and their psychiatric, as well as cognitive needs.

Hospital Setting:

Most likely, in a hospital setting, you will be responsible for conducting discharge planning. A discharge plan is needed to release a patient, with usually some type of follow-up care.

Discharge planning should occur on the first day of admittance. The reason for this procedure is two-fold: First of all. you need to have a plan in place of what a client might require based on his/her diagnosis/symptoms. Secondly, logistically speaking, discharge planners tend to be overloaded with cases. Therefore, they need to start working right away in order to be able to service everyone in an orderly and timely fashion.

This is also when self-determination might come into play. Based on the situation, you will either need to respect a client's choices with his/her medical care (if he/she is not mentally alert), or you may need to provide safeguards for that individual. The safeguards would come in the form of "family members, legal guardians or authorized community representatives". In other words, family members, legal guardians or community representatives would have to sign Informed Consent on the clients' behalf.

You may also be involved with Advanced Directives and determining the clients' choices on end-of-life decisions.

Working in a Hospice:

A hospice is a facility for individuals that are ill and are often diagnosed with terminal illness. Their medical symptoms cannot be managed at home; therefore, a hospice is indicated. Therefore, the type of work that is involved will be delicate.

Responsibilities could include:

- Coordinating with medical personnel

- Discharge planning (Even though patients may be diagnosed with a terminal illness, they may still be transferred to other placements, such as a nursing home, or their own home.

- Participating in team meetings where the progress of the patients is discussed

- Communication with families regarding the medical status of the client

- Providing psychoeducation to families regarding medical conditions

- Funeral arrangements (obtaining verbal consent to have the client released into the funeral home, notifying the funeral homes)

- Lessening family burden. The SW will act as a liaison (go-between the medical professionals and the family, the client and the family, the funeral home and the family, etc.)

Important term in hospice care: - Chaplain: A member of the clergy in a private chapel or institution.

Final Note on Practice Settings:

It is impossible to account for every practicum situation that may appear on the exam, however the above-mentioned information lists the mostly commonly used practicum settings.

Chapter 25

Social Acts and Policies:

We have already learned about some aspects of social policy. However, often, social distress or different types of global incidents may lead to a new or a different policy. It is important for a social worker to be aware of these policies, so they know how to protect their clients' rights.

Some Important Acts to be Aware of:

ADA - The American with Disabilities Act (1990): This Act protects individuals with Disabilities (physical and Intellectual). The crux of the Act is that workers having disabilities are entitled to reasonable accommodations. An example of a reasonable accommodation could be an ergonomic keyboard, for someone who has Carpal Tunnel Syndrome. This is the reason why you are asked so many questions on job applications. Employers want to make sure that if you are disabled, you are afforded reasonable accommodations and also want to make sure that you are the right fit for the job, depending on the type of tasks involved.

Title VI: Civil Rights Act of 1964: No person should be discriminated against, based on color, religion, race, ethnicity. No person should be excluded from national rights based on the above factors.

HIPAA - Protection of rights/confidentiality of medical records.

Older Americans Act of 1965: Providing resources/services to older Americans.

Child Abuse Prevention and Treatment Act of 1974: Provides funding for investigations, prosecution of child abuse.

(Side Note: The goal of children in foster families is Permanency Planning - meaning reuniting with biological parents (provided they are fit to raise the child) or planning for a permanent home - adoption.)

Indian Child Welfare Act of 1978: - The tribe is responsible for the care/welfare of any situation involving an American Indian child.

The Education for All Handicapped Children Act of 1975: - All children with handicaps/disabilities are entitled to free education.

No Child Left Behind: (2001): Schools are required to be accountable for the performance of all children whether or not they have disabilities. All schools are also required to perform routine assessments to gauge the progress of students.

P.L. 94-142 (Public Law 94-142:): - This policy states that public schools that receive federal funding must provide equal access to handicapped children, as well as a free meal.

In conjunction with the topic of Acts, a short section should be devoted to Advanced Directives: What is an Advanced Directive? This is a legal document that identifies your final wishes and who will be responsible for carrying them out.

A living will be suggested, as often, in the cases of a coma, or an individual on life support, the decision of his/her remaining life choices is left up in the air. In the case of a living will/ a health care proxy it is very clear what the decision is and who will enforce/carry out this decision. The health care proxy is a legal document in which the client appoints a person to make healthcare decision on his/her behalf, in case they are not able to. For example, it could be a family member, loved one, etc.

You as a Social Worker may encounter this situation in a hospice. A hospice is a facility for individuals with serious and terminal illnesses.

On many occasions, there have been situations in which families fought over medical decisions of their loved ones, who were not capable of making an informed decision. A living will eliminate all that confusion and is almost like a "prescription" of what a client wants.

Chapter 26

Psychological Testing

During the assessment phase of a client's treatment process, testing may serve as a useful tool. For example, if you are trying to assess the extent of his/her depression, the Beck Depression Inventory may be used.

If you are trying to assess the clients' adaptive skills, you may want to enlist the help of a WAIS- R. Even if you're not administering any test to your client, you may want to be familiar with testing and its influence on a person's intellect, behavior, personality.

For personality assessment, the Rorschach Test/ Draw- A - Person, MMPI, Myers Briggs are also used to help the social worker define/explore a client's personality.

Myers-Briggs: Essentially, this test examines the level of Introversion vs. Extroversion in a person.

MMPI (Think **P for Personality**) - The Minnesota Multiphasic Personality Inventory: - This exam assesses an individual on multiple of categories and tests out the pathologies that a person may have.

Thematic Apperception Test (TAT) - the individual constructs a story based on a set of pictures that are presented.

Beck Depression Inventory: 21 questions to assess the severity of one's depression.

Wechsler Intelligence Scale - assess the cognitive ability of an individual (often used in persons with Intellectual Disabilities); there are multiple categories of this scale, and it is a long test.

Vineland Adaptive Scale: - tests individuals' adaptive abilities (also commonly used with people with Intellectual Disabilities.)

Chapter 27

Final Note

There is a lot of information related to the practice of Social Work.

This exam is meant for you to be familiar and knowledgeable with the topics that were discussed in this book. You don't have to know them verbatim! You need to know enough to pick them out in an answer on the exam. Remember, SAFETY AND HEALTH are first! (Maslow's hierarchy of needs). Assessment is a crucial step. You are a mandated reporter in instances of Alleged Abuse - Elder, Child, etc.; Do no Harm! and Duty to Warn intended victims of possible crimes against them! /Tarasoff Act; Prioritize ASSESSMENT / Allow the group.... In Community...........Identify the needs of the community FIRST.

I know that this exam can seem anxiety-producing and overwhelming, but it is within your reach. The more prepared you are, the better you will feel with mastering the exam.

IF ALL FAILS, PLEASE GO AND VIEW JUST ABOUT EVERY EPISODE OF "LITTLE HOUSE". It is my all-time favorite show and every episode dealt with situations in a Social-Work way type of way. :) "You'll see exactly what I'm talking about when you watch."(That's a personal and somewhat professional recommendation.) :)

(LAW **and ORDER SVU)** is also way on track with their techniques. I particularly like the episode **"Retro"** in the 10th Season, as it **discusses medical neglect and self-determination**. Pay close attention to "Informed Consent/Mandated reports/Rape Kit - Rule Out Health.) I hope you found this guide useful, and I wish you the BEST OF L

GOOD LUCK ON YOUR EXAM!

Chapter 28

Tutoring Services:

I conduct Group and Individual Tutoring Services at an affordable rate. I also hold live and Zoom workshops that you can be a part of. Send me your email for a schedule of upcoming Workshops. I have a high success rate in helping people pass.

If you want more information, you can look me up on any Social Media Sites under my Name. You can also contact me at: APerlin7@gmail.com.

Thank you for purchasing and reading this book! I am hopeful that you will find it very useful for your knowledge in social work and in preparation for the Exam. Good Luck on the Exam and in your Career! This is a very notable, noble career and I commend every Social Worker for undergoing with the educational and vocational requirements in order to continue servicing others. I appreciate you and am proud to call you, my colleagues! May your career be successful and may all your clients be helped by your miraculous work. Thank you.

Test Answers and Explanations.

Test Answers and Explanations.

1. The right answer is: B- In the Code of Ethics "Conflicts of Interests" standard, it is stated that Social Workers should avoid relationships with former clients if there is potential for harm. The client had attachment issues. Therefore, it is not advisable to enter into a relationship with that client. The Social Worker does not need to completely avoid the former client. He/she can say a polite "Hello" and gracefully excuse him/herself.

2. - D - The symptoms here are consistent with Depression. However, the fact that it lasts for more than 2 years, it is diagnosable as Persistent Depressive Disorder/ (former Dysthymia).

3. - C - The likely diagnosis that's described here is borderline personality disorder. Rapproachment is a stage in Mahler that's related to poor boundaries/poor sense of attachment. In "Rapproachment", the child individuates/shows independence from the mother. Based on how the mother handles it, could set up the potential for poor or healthy boundaries, therefore possibly resulting in borderline personality disorder.

4. - C - This is called the "Duty to warn" or the Tarasoff Act. This Act resulted out of a real situation, in which a psychiatrist saw a patient that disclosed to him that they were about to harm somebody. The psychiatrist did not warn the victim. The patient went through with the plan. Then, the psychiatrist was sued because he did not go to any lengths to warn the intended victim. If you don't find the victim or his/her loved ones/friends, you need to call the authorities. Confidentiality does not apply in this matter. The Tarasoff Act is not upheld in every state. However, the exam is likely to use it as a nation-wide approach. If the answers identify "varies by state", that response would be accurate.

5. C - Health Insurance Portability Accountability Act.

6. D - Generalized Anxiety Disorder; Symptoms of restlessness, insomnia, lack of concentration, muscle tension must last for 6 months and are categorized under Generalized Anxiety Disorder.

7. - C - Confronting is not a good idea. It denotes a negative connotation. Therefore, the answer is C. You should not tell the supervisor right away, as it may not be alcohol you're smelling. If the colleague continues to have alcohol on his breath or dismisses you when you approach him after a few days, then the situation needs to be reported to the supervisor.

8. D- Identity vs. Identity Diffusion/Role Confusion - In this situation, this stage, according to Erikson is not resolved. An individual is 45 and still continues to dress up like Lady Gaga. If she was a teenager, it would then be more acceptable.

9. -C. This is Kohlberg's Theory of Moral Development. The first stage is the pre conventional stage. It suggests that the individual/child's sense of morality is based on what avoids punishment.

10. - C. Pre-operational stage. This is Piaget's 2nd Stage of Cognitive Development. In this stage, the child does not yet comprehend the concept of irreversibility; has not begun to count numbers, etc.

11. - C. Autistic Spectrum Disorder; ASD is characterized by impaired social skills. The child in this situation keeps to himself. He also exhibits ritualistic behaviors, such as rocking, standing in one spot and arranging things in a certain manner.

12. - C - Profound Intellectual Disability. This is the lowest level of functioning in Intellectual Disability (formerly Mental Retardation). The adult in question is not able to perform ADL skills, even with prompting.

13. - D - You cannot report the situation to the co-workers or the supervisor. The reason for that is that it is possible that the supervisor and/or co-workers instigated the alleged abuse. It is not necessary to speak to the woman more, as she already stopped speaking.

14. - Power Struggle. This is a Couples Theory question. Beyonce and JayZ both want control of the finances.

15. - D - Reaction Formation. Reaction formation is a defense mechanism, in which an individual turns an unacceptable, uncomfortable feeling into its direct opposite.

16. - D - The correct answer is D, as there are more opportunities for the actor to relapse within a year. During the year, there are holidays, events, more connections with prior friends, etc. The actor may relapse after a year, but the likelihood is that he will relapse within a year.

17. - C - This is consistent with Operant Conditioning. Operant Conditioning states that reinforcing/rewarding a behavior will likely result in more instances of this behavior. "The Law of Effect" is formulated by Thorndike.

18. - C - The SW should discuss this case with a supervisor. It is a case of Counter transference, in which the SW exhibits feelings for the client. The SW Supervisor will help the employee "work through" the feelings or have suggestions on how to handle the conflict. Alternatively, the case may be re-assigned.

19. - C. - Hispanic - American. The key phrases here are: Excessively emotional, does not need therapy and candle rituals. The Hispanic- American population have a tendency to be perceived as excessively emotional, to refuse therapy and to engage in other forms of support, such as candle rituals, rather than social services or therapy.

20. - D - In any situation where there are UNEXPLAINED, UNKNOWN OR SUSPICIOUS cuts/scrapes, marks, the SW needs to report IMMEDIATELY.

21. - C - There are usually guidelines in each agency, as far as tips, gifts, etc. for the social worker. For some agencies, the cut-off point is $25. If a client brings in a small gift, such as a tray of cookies, it is not an outrageously expensive gift and can be accepted. Additionally, the client also does not derive a benefit from it. If the SW refuses, the client may feel offended. If the gift presents any cash value, it needs to be declined in a polite manner.

22. - D - The answer is D because the gift is highly inappropriate, and the SW also need to discuss the case with the Supervisor. The male client may have developed

sexual/romantic feels for the SW, and it may not be a good idea for them to continue sessions together.

23. - C- The stage of "Trust vs. Mistrust" is unresolved, as the woman never bonded with the child. The child/now-grown woman has now developed a sense of distrust with others.

24. A. - Homogenous means: Similar, in terms of Age, Interests, Educational level, etc. It is thought of as more beneficial to have homogenous clients in a group together, because they are more able to relate to one another.

25. D. The answer is Social Planning. The SW is gathering information through research to develop a Diabetes Awareness Training.

26. C. - The answer is Triangulation, as the family brings in a third party (Tri) to speak for them.

27. C. - Substance Abuse - because the man's drinking has not affected his job yet. Substance dependence is when Tolerance is developed. Also, withdrawal occurs, as a result of stopping the substance.

28. - C. It is important to involve the remaining staff in the decision-making process. The Administrator should get input from the remaining employees, as to what procedures/actions should help the division. The remaining employees are in the front lines, so they are more aware of the problem and its possible resolution.

29. A. - The answer is A - Reflection. The SW is reflecting the problem back to the client. "Partialization" - means breaking down the problem into more manageable parts; "Listening with intent" - in not a technique and "Clarification" - means that you may be rephrasing or re-asking the question for more clarity.

30. D. - This is the most ethical answer. With A, you're not really answering the questions and possibly the information; with B - you haven't taken the exam yet and are not sure if you will pass.; with C - you are misrepresenting yourself and discrediting the license.

31. C. - The man has not resolved the Intimacy vs. Isolation stage and has also not resolved the Generative vs. Stagnation stage. The key phrase here is that "he is not worried about the children's future at present."

32. D - Even though it's a woman in her 40's, she is adopting/imitating the opinions of others'. Therefore, she has not passed the "Identity vs. Role confusion."

33. B. - Initiative vs. guilt. The child is taking initiative/exploring the office and answering questions.

34.- C - The woman has developed good social connections. She has passed Intimacy vs. Isolation.

35- A - The key here is a few phrases. The child is 6 and is having problems in school. He is also not making friends. He's displaying anxiety over school. He is in the "Inferiority part of the Industry vs. Inferiority" stage.

36- B- Ego Integrity vs. Despair. This is the last stage of Erikson, in which an individual does a life review. If they are satisfied with their life, they are in "Integrity". If they have regrets over their life, they are in despair.

37 - B - Autonomy vs. Shame and Doubt. The child is connected /attached to family members, as well as displaying appropriate developmental milestones. He is "Autonomous/ or independent".

38 - C - Trust vs. Mistrust. The woman never developed a sense of Trust in her infancy stages. Therefore, she is distrustful or suspicious of others.

39. - C - This is Freud's Theory of Psychosexual development. In the Latency stage, the child (6-12) moves away from the sexual aspect of pleasure-seeking and moves into the social stage (making friends).

40 - D - This is pertaining to Mahler's Object Relations Theory. Differentiation is the stage in which, the child is individuating by crawling, but the mother is still around him.

41 - B - This is Kohlberg's Theory of Moral Development. The individual is influenced by his peers and his/her moral compass are directed by what his/her friends say.

42 - C - In Freud's Phallic Stage, the child is more vulnerable to being exploited because he/she is not aware of his private parts and what they do.

43 - D- Groupthink refers to a concept in Group Therapy, in which the group members start to think and talk alike.

44 - B - The symptoms are reflective of Major Depressive Disorder and the duration of 2 weeks is accurate.

45 - B - The woman "Undoes what she did".

46 - C - The dependent variable is the outcome. The independent variable is the intervention/what's being changed.

47 - A - Klonozepam/ or its generic name Klonopin is used to treat Anxiety.

48 - C - The ADA states that people with Disabilities are entitled to Reasonable Accommodations from their employers.

49 - C - We want to respect the man's self-determination, so we don't need to explore Home Health Aide Options, as he does not fully need them. We don't need to explore his ability to make decisions on his own. We don't need to assess his Collateral/family resources, as he is only seeking assistance for ambulation problems.

50 - A - This is a "Safety First question." Even though the first word says, "Refer"; all the other options don't apply. She needs to get to a safe place and then she can obtain resources to find a job.

51 - C - We need to keep treating him "pro bono" or free, but we do not want to treat him indefinitely. We still need to be compensated for our services, so we need to find him a Free Clinic.

52 - C- The technique we are seeking is the "Miracle question", which asks the client "What would happen if all your problems were solved tomorrow"? The therapy that is being used is "Solution-focused therapy.

53 - C - Practicing. This is the later stage of Mahler, in which the child is now more independent and is able to walk, but the mom is still around him.

54 - B - In this stage of Mahler, the child has internalized the mom. He knows that she is coming back.

55 - D - This stage speaks to boundaries. If the child tries to separate from the mom by walking away but continues to look back to make sure she's there, that is "Rapproachment".

56 - A - First stage of Mahler is Autistic.

57 - B - Symbiosis. The child is still connected to the mom but has begun to see that she is a different being.

58 - B – "Unconditional positive regard" means constantly accepting the woman.

59 - B - Person- centered therapy uses the concept of Unconditional Positive Regard.

60 - B - Confrontation is when the client's actions may not match up his words and the SW points out this inconsistency.

61 - C - Projection: Placing your feelings onto someone else.

62 - B - Piaget: Sensori-Motor: Learning with the senses.

63 - A - Piaget: Formal Operations: The adolescent is able to use thinking to plan/strategize.

64 - C - Concrete Operations - Piaget. In Concrete Operations, the child is able to use the concept of Conservation.

65 - D - Superego; The conscience; The superego mediates between the Id and the Ego and arrives at a socially acceptable solution.

66 - D - Sublimation. This is a defense mechanism in which the individual channels an unacceptable/uncomfortable emotion into a positive action.

67 - C - Intellectualization: A defense mechanism, in which you are using logic to dismiss an uncomfortable emotion.68 - A - Rationalization: Making an excuse.

68 - A - Rationalization: Making up excuses.

69 - B - Introjection: Taking an uncomfortable emotion onto/into yourself.

70 - C - Bargaining: Making deals with God to bring the loved one back.

71 - B - Post Conventional: The stage in which the individual is able to understand why laws/rules are necessary.

72 - B - Caretaker: The person in the family unit, in which one individual takes care of everyone else.

73 - D - Confrontation: Pointing out inconsistencies.

74 - B - Regression: Reverting to a past state.

75 - A - Rationalization: Making up excuses.

76 - C - Social Action: Acting on behalf of the individuals, as they are incapable of helping themselves.

77 - A - Social Planning: Research

78 - C - Vineland Adaptive Scale: - Assessing adaptive functioning.

79 - B - Conversion disorder is a disorder in which there is no direct physical cause for the symptoms.

80 - B- Emotional Fusion: This is a process, in which the family is enmeshed and a departure by one member results in a feeling of betrayal by the family.

81 - D - PICA: This is a disorder, in which persons eat inedible objects.

82 - C - You cannot begin the experiment without the subjects' consent.

83 - B- Secondary Prevention, in which the condition already occurred and now measures must be taken to prevent further damage.

84 - B - Bipolar II: This is marked by hypomania (lasts for 4 days) and Major Depressive Disorder.

85 - C - Social Anxiety Disorder. This is a disorder, in which the individual is extremely uncomfortable around others and is afraid of being judged by others.

86 - B – Grandiose delusions: is a condition, in which an individual believes that he/she is being followed/ there is a plot against them, etc.

87 - B - Social Exchange Theory postulates that the individual will choose to either stay or end the relationship based upon the benefits/disadvantages of the relationship.

88 - C - Arab-American woman wear a hijab/head dress and also cannot be in close proximity to a man.

89 - A - In this case, the man is respecting Cultural Differences by not shaking the womens' hands.

90 - C - In Narrative Therapy, the client is asked to use writing as a therapeutic technique.

91 - B If there is a bruise, you must report it as an alleged abuse situation.

92 - C - The Diagnostic Statistical Manual of Mental Disorders (fifth edition.)

93 - B - Schizophrenia. Risperidone or Risperidal is an anti-psychotic.

94 - B - Validate before contacting the supervisor.

95 - D - Conflicts of Interests.

96 - C - Coercive Power: It is when the agent has control over punishments.

97 - C - You must secure the services of a professional translator.

98 - B - You need to explain to the teenager that he cannot join as the group has already started and it would be disruptive to other group members if a new person joins. In order to further support him, you need to refer him to a grief counselor, while he is waiting for another group to start.

99 - A – Historionic Personality Disorder.

100 - A - posttraumatic stress disorder (Night mates, re-living the incident, etc.)

101 - D- Intellectualization. Instead of processing her feelings, the young lady is using an intellectual tactic to cope with the situation.

102 - B- Brief Psychotic Disorder

103 - D- obsessive compulsive disorder

104 - B - borderline personality disorder

105 - C - Oppositional Defiant Disorder

106 -   B - Adderal

107   - B - Trazadone

108 - C- Normalize the daughter's feelings.

109 - B - Respect cultural differences and self-determination. This situation does not constitute medical neglect, as there is no life-threatening condition or deterioration current condition.

110 - C- Prozac is an anti-depressant.

111 - B - The client who is diagnosed with Intellectual Disabilities may not be able to communicate that he/she is in physical discomfort. Therefore, the initial assessment should include a Physical Examination. Concurrently, referrals may be part of the Assessment process to pinpoint more information.

112 - B - We cannot treat a client who is intoxicated. Also, we cannot assess the level of their inebriation. Therefore, the safest option is to arrange for a family member or a friend to have her picked up. This is done for safety purposes, so the client does not proceed to drive herself home or gets into any other accident.

113 - B- The purpose is to have the different disciplines come to an agreement regarding the client's best possible treatment.

114 - B - This goes to the "Interruption of Services" standard in the Code of Ethics. The SW must take reasonable steps to secure continuity of care.

115 C - This would be a Conflict of Interests.

116 - D - This is the standard that allows the client to have reasonable access to records if there is no potential for harm.

117- C - This is a billing issue according to the Code of Ethics. It would be fraudulent to falsify documentation.

118 - A - It is a socially acceptable practice to shake hands. Similarly, you may also be offering a teaching moment to the client by redirecting him/her to shake hands.

119 - B - "Gestalt therapy is known for the "Empty Chair technique".

120 - C - The experimental Group is the one that receives the actual treatment.

121 - D - Michelle must gauge the interests of the community. This is the first part of the Community Organizing effort.

122 - B- The mediator is the person that settles disputes.

123 - A - Macro- level Advocacy includes policies, program development and evaluation and Administrative Practices.

124 - B - "The Social Action " part of the Community Social Work model includes the active part of the process. The fact that individuals are unable to advocate for themselves would indicate that the Social Worker has to do it for them.

125 - B- Longitudinal studies concern themselves with studies spanning across time.

126 - C- The increased energy could indicate that the client has more strength to go through with the attempt.

127- A- Pre-affiliation.

128 - B- The Quantitative Design includes numbers.

129 - C - AB design

130 - C- The mode is the number that appears the most often.

131 - A - A Stratified group involves only one "strata" (location, age group, sex, etc.)

132 - A - Conflict theory is the notion that there may arise a natural hostility between community members. This may be due to limited resources or exclusion in certain groups.

133 - C- Unconditional positive regard - means continual acceptance of the client.

134 - C - Authoritative

135 - C - Ethnocentrism - the belief that one's culture is superior to others.

136- D - Agoraphobia - In Greek, this means, fear of the marketplace; - In social work, this term is used to describe an extreme fear of being outside and around others.

137 - B - Mascot - The mascot is the family member that uses humor to mask underlying tensions/problems in the family.

138 - D - The Indian Welfare of 1978.

139 - B- The Myers Briggs Test is the scale of Introversion/vs. Extroversion.

140 - B - Conflicts of Interests

141-- B- Privacy and Confidentiality

142 - B - Deny the request.

143- C - This exception is only allowed in very restricted circumstances. If it is the accepted practice/norm of the Community, the SW can agree to this arrangement with the Informed Consent of the client.

144 - D - A legal representative must advocate on behalf of the client who can't make decisions.

145 - A - This refers to the Competence standard in the Code of Ethics. In this situation, the person must refer to a professional that is well-versed in that area.

146. - A- Heroin withdrawal symptoms are associated with restlessness and bone pain.

147. - B - Suboxone is one of the treatment choices for heroin addiction.

148 - C - In cases of high suicidal risk, the client needs to be encouraged or coerced to go to the hospital.

149 - B - Even though this is a teenager, she is still our client, and we must respect her self-determination.

150 - D - Self-determination is key here, as well. The man is capable of making decisions; therefore, he has a right to alternative treatments as methods for treating his cancer.

151- A - The next step after completing a thorough Assessment is to develop a treatment plan with the client.

152 - B - As the client has suffered with a stroke, he may lose functional ability in some of his physical organs and body parts. Therefore, he might require crutches, home health aide care and outpatient service options.

153 - D - The discharge process must start as soon as the client is admitted to the hospital.

154 - D - Employees tend to suffer from burn-out when the structure of the agency and their policies are not in line with employee standards. Therefore, the SW Administrator must change the policies associated with the benefits that have to do with employee benefits and awareness.

155 - A - The Initiator is the person or group that first recognizes that a problem exists.

156 - C - The SW should complete a Suicide Risk Assessment. The client has suffered a great loss and is implying possible suicidal ideation.

157 - B - This is an Administration question. The reason that conflict could exist is due to misunderstandings regarding different roles of the disciplines. Often, employees argue as they are not aware of each other's responsibilities in the different domain.

158 - C - Human Resources need to interview employees to find out about their job responsibilities. This will give them a more accurate picture of the position and they may be able to write a better Job description to a prospective hire.

159 - D - This is a Macro question. It refers to steps in Macro Change Efforts. The tactic of "Collective Action" is considered a confrontational tactic, in which boycotts or sit-ins may be involved in order to get the change effort across.

160- B - Although other methods might be important, the first role of the Social Worker is to establish rapport. He/she may do that by acknowledging feelings. The SW should allow the client opportunity to talk about his current loss.

161 - A - This is both a Supervision and a Code of Ethics question. According to the Code of Ethics, it is not ethical for a professional to keep working if they are under severe duress. It may cause them to do their job improperly. The SW Supervisor should encourage the SW to take some time off and return when she is feeling better.

162 - C- The best course of Action is to invite the Psychiatrist to discuss the treatment option. It is not indicated to involve the parents yet, prior to making a firm decision on the treatment choice.

163 - D - The mother has the right to change the information in her child's record, as per F.E.R.P.A. laws.

164 - B - This is a Macro change question. On the Macro level of Intervention, the SW needs to advocate for the unethical reason of denying the client employment.

165 - B- Both parties involved were non-consenting. Therefore, they do not understand the ramifications of the sexual activity, pregnancy and the termination of pregnancy. Therefore, a legal guardian must advocate on their behalf.

166 - B- It is the right thing to do to seek alternative arrangements. This is referred to in the Code of ethics as the "Transfer of Services".

167- C- "Holding a fund-raising event and inviting the land developers" would kill two birds with one stone. First of all, the Community Social Worker would have an opportunity to involve the opposition (Co-optation). Secondly, they would have the opportunity to raise funds for the homeless shelter.

168- B- By holding a "Block Party", the community social workers would raise awareness regarding the "Intellectual Disabled client population."

169- B- The null hypothesis is the principle that there is no relationship between the independent variable and the dependent variable. The experimenter would want to "reject the null hypothesis" in order to attempt to prove that there is a relationship between the independent variable and the dependent variable.

170 - C- This is a community question. This would show an effort in resolving the opposition by inviting them for a meeting, as well as providing psychoeducation.

171- C- The first step is to gauge the interests of the community, as you're working in conjunction with them.

172 - C- One of the rules of the supervisor is educating the client. Therefore, the Supervisor would offer strategies on how the supervisee can handle the situation by him/herself.

173- D- There is an incongruence between the student's previous academic performance/behavior and the current issues of truancy, as well as lack of concentration. Therefore, we must deduce that a change has occurred. In order to best aid the student, a psychological evaluation is warranted to see if the change may be attributable to another presenting situation. (ADHD, Learning disability, etc.)

174 - B- This is a possible case of "statutory rape". Therefore, the SW must consult the state regulations as far as their legislative practices on this matter. If the incident constitutes "Statutory rape", it must be reported to the proper authorities.

175 - C - "Do away with" is an ambiguous statement. It could mean different things. Therefore, the SW must clarify what it means to the individual.

176 - D- Since the man reported confusion and especially "rapid weight loss", this could indicate a medical diagnosis. Therefore, the SW must refer the individual to the physician.

177 - B- That statement could imply "Unrealistic expectations". The Social Worker wants the client to have a clear understanding of the treatment process. Therefore, the Social Worker needs to clarify the client/social worker expectations as early as possible.

178 - B- The Social Worker is unable to discuss any information about the client, without informed consent. The SW is not even allowed to reveal whether the client is attending the sessions. Similarly, (s)he can't discuss the client's name.

179 - A - Since this is an older woman and her experience consists of reminiscing about her past, we must allow her to do so.

180- C - We must acknowledge his feelings of resistance.

181 - C - Since this is a mandated client, we must report any attendance issues to the parole officer.

182 - B - The Beck Depression Inventory Scale.

183 - D - It is necessary to use any means of escape if the Social Worker feels (s)he is in danger.

184- C- It is acceptable to use any documented information a Social Worker has, in cases of lawsuits.

185 - C- It is necessary to advise the client of the risks associated with Tele-therapy, as there could be possible safety concerns.

186 - C - The only practical choice is to limit the number of holiday parties. It may be illegal in some cases to reduce employees' wages; it is unethical to eliminate the clients' music program (Client services are not to be affected during budget cuts.); and some employees might rely on bonuses in order to help them with their expenses. Therefore, this would not be a prudent choice.

187 - C - Since we are already in the evaluation phase, the best strategy would be to conduct an external audit. During an external audit, the consultants are objective and would be able to give the most accurate information on the programs' success.

188 - B - Refer to Alona Perlin's "Priority Triangle". The symptoms are all indicative of substance use disorder, namely, problems at work, sleeping problems and extreme mood shifts. Therefore, you would want to "inquire more into the increase in alcohol use".

189 - C - Cyclothymia is consistent with these symptoms due to the 2-year time frame.

190 - D- Avoidant Personality Disorder is indicative of individuals' who are interested in forming relationships, but push them away, "avoid" them, due to a fear of rejection. "Schizotypal Personality Disorder" suggests odd, eccentric behavior, as well as the presence of magical thinking. "Schizoaffective Disorder" - is symptoms of schizophrenia, as well as emotionality/mood disorder and "Anti-social Personality Disorder" is experienced by individuals with no regard for human life; exhibit criminal-like behavior and show no remorse.

191- B- Repression. Repression is the defense mechanism that works to block out painful memories or traumatic situations.

192 - C - When it comes to "end of life decisions", it is necessary to defer to Advanced Directives, such as the living will / DNR. ("Do not Resuscitate" instructions).

193 - C - The best approach is to ask the woman directly.

194 - D- It is unethical to take credit for the ideas of coworkers, as per the Code of Ethics. Therefore, the best choice would be to explain that this was a team effort.

195 - A - "Storming" corresponds to the "Power and Control" stage, as this is the stage in which groups members may start to cultivate roles of dominator/vs. passive participants.

196 - B - This is a concept developed by Piaget. It means, modifying our schemas (mental representations). to account for new information. Assimilation means modifying new information to fit into our schemas. (Question 201 is created because of a repeat question earlier in the book.)

197- C - While there are several possible indicators of sexual abuse, the best indicator is "Excessive masturbation".

198- C- Statistically, older white males have the highest risk factor for suicide, especially if they have access to a gun.

199 - C- It may not be feasible for members to join at the designated time. Therefore, it is important to ask them their time and date preferences.

200 - B- Vivitrol is used to treat Opiate Addiction.

(**Note**: Some questions were repeated, so I'm adding on these additional questions)

201 – A- As per the Code of Ethics (Privacy standard), we have the option to ask the court that the disclosed information is protected from public records and is kept under seal.

202 – D- Cogentin is used to take away the side effects of anti-psychotic medication.

203- C- Tardive Dyskenesia is characterized by jerky, involuntary movements and a protruding tongue.

204- B- The median is considered the mid-point on the graph

Recommended Reading: This is my favorite pleasure- reading material relating to Social Work: If you'd like, you can check it out after the exam. Alternatively, if you have plenty of time to prepare for the exam, you can pick it up as research. It is also touching, interesting and may be instrumental in understanding Social Work more.

1- **Three Little Words (2009)** _ by Ashley Rhodes-Courter (A true-life story of a foster care survivor.)

2- **Finding Fish (2001)** by Antwone Quenton Fisher (A memoir of "Baby Boy Fisher", depicting a horrifying childhood, as well as his experience in foster care placement.)

3- **Dreams from My Father** (A Story of Race and Inheritance): (2004) by Barack Obama (This autobiography describes President Obama's beginnings in the political. arena.

4- **My Life: (2004)** by Bill Clinton (1000 pages - yes 1000 pps., but it's worth the read) (Bill Clinton's autobiography).

5- **She's Come Undone (1992):** by Wally Lamb: Obesity; abuse; mental illness

Recommended Movies:

1 - "Forrest Gump": Tom Hanks/ - for info: on an individual with Intellectual Disabilities (has more entertaining value, however, :)

2- "Rain Man": Dustin Hoffman/Tom Cruise: - for info. on individuals with Autistic Spectrum Disorder

3- "I Am Sam" - (amazing performance by Sean Penn): - for info. individuals with Autistic Spectrum Disorder

4- "A Beautiful Mind": Russell Crowe: - for info. on persons with Schizophrenia

5- "Eve's Bayou"; Diahann Carroll; Samuel J. Jackson; - for insight into sexual abuse

6 - "Awakenings": Robin Williams: Robert DeNiro (how can you go wrong with that combination? for info. on aspects of Catatonia and Parkinson's disease

7 - "Girl, Interrupted" - Angelina Jolie/Winona Ryder, For info. on patients in mental institutions

8 - "Shawshank Redemption" - Morgan Freeman/Tim Robbins; - Prison Culture

9 - "Just Mercy" - Michael B. Jordan; - Prison culture/lack of proper legal representation.

10 - "The Help" - Viola Davis/Octavia Spence - Racial disparities

11- "Precious" - Gabourney Sidibe - Abuse/H.I.V., etc.

12 - "The Color Purple" - Oprah Winfrey/ Whoopi Goldberg (Also, how can you go wrong with that combination? They are both fantastic in this movie) - Abuse/bigotry

13- "The Intern" - Robert DeNiro: Anne Hathaway - a very poignant film about aging.

Recommended Current TV Programs:

1 - "For Life" - Nicholas Pinnock: 'based on the life of Aaron Wallace; - Prison culture/racial conflicts

2- "Empire" - Terrence Howard, Taraji P. Henson; (LGBTQ issues; some info. on prison culture)

3- "Self-Made" - Octavia Spencer; (Women's empowerment)

4- " This is Us" - Sterling K. Brown; Milo Ventimiglia; Mandy Moore (Anxiety; obesity, adoption issues; community, etc.)

5- "The Assassination of Gianni Versace" - American Crime Story - Darren Criss (amazing job as the leading man"); Ricky Martin, Penelope Cruz; - Psychopathology

6- "Little Fires Everywhere" - Kerry Washington, Reese Witherspoon/Joshua Jackson - Social/racial tensions; issues of motherhood.

These are just some of my favorite movies and series; some people swear by other fantastic ones, but I either haven't gotten around to them or they didn't resonate with me.

Just think, you'll have something to look forward to upon PASSING THE EXAM!

Once again, **GOOD LUCK** and my **CONGRATULATIONS IN ADVANCE!!**

Made in the USA
Middletown, DE
08 September 2023